The Housing Act 2(
Residential Letting

A Practical Guide

Francis Davey & David Smith

Acknowledgment

Crown copyright material is reproduced with the permission of the Controller of HMSO and the Queen's Printer for Scotland.

Please note: References to the masculine include, where appropriate, the feminine.

Published by the Royal Institution of Chartered Surveyors (RICS)

Surveyor Court

Westwood Business Park

Coventry CV4 8JE

UK

www.ricsbooks.com

No responsibility for loss or damage caused to any person acting or refraining from action as a result of the material included in this publication can be accepted by the author or RICS.

ISBN 978 1 84219 405 8

Typeset in Great Britain by Columns Design Ltd, Reading, Berks

Printed in Great Britain by Alden Group, Oxford

This publication is printed on environmentally friendly paper from sustainable forests.

Contents

Preface

It is a pleasure to write a Preface to this important new practical work on housing law which has been prepared specially for surveyors and other experts who regularly advise on housing and rented accommodation. This work focuses on the enormous legal and policy changes that were introduced by the *Housing Act* 2004. Although this work appears some four years after the Act received Royal Assent, it is nevertheless timely; the commencement timetable has been slow, for one thing. It is only this year that the Act will be fully in force. A further reason why this new book is so timely is that the authors have been able to take account of the early implementation of the Act, such as the decisions of the Residential Property Tribunals, and the ways in which local authority environmental health officers are exercising their new powers and responsibilities.

This Housing Act is aimed primarily at private sector housing, and it is part of a policy of improving conditions for those living in such rented accommodation. It is well-known that, as a result of various changes made to the legal position of private landlords and tenants, private rented accommodation has become largely deregulated. Many tenants are not in a position to realistically enforce action to ameliorate poor housing standards. Perhaps the move to market rents and the greater investment in the sector may help its improvement over the long term, perhaps not. In practice it may well be that the new measures, particularly those in Parts 1–4 of the Bill which give both new and revised powers to local authority officers, will exert a positive effect on the sector.

Landlords and tenants will need expert guidance on the workings of the new Act. As the authors point out, it is not just the Act itself that must be studied; one must also take full account of the huge volume of regulations and official guidance as well. Part I of the Act introduces a new way of dealing with the worst conditions in rented housing – the new so-called HHSRS – that has been portrayed as a more logical and fairer way of focusing the attentions of EHOs and those who let and those who rent. For those individuals who share accommodation, the measures in Part 2 which apply to houses in multiple occupation and for those who own and rent them may prove important. Regulating HMOs is not new: but the 2004 Act focuses attention on the properties which are of greater risk to occupiers. The Act also gives local authorities powers to intervene, including radical new powers to take over the management and control of accommodation including powers in relation to empty dwellings. It seems already to be the case that many authorities are using their new EDMO powers quite extensively.

As the Government stated in the various papers which led to the Housing Bill and during the parliamentary debates, these measures are aimed at that part of the private rented sector – a small part – where housing conditions are poor. Even so, good landlords may also have to deal with the Act. Indeed all landlords have to comply with the new tenancy deposit scheme.

This reinforces the point made earlier in this Preface, that private landlords and their tenants will need good professional advice. This will often include advice from surveyors on housing conditions. All property professionals could benefit from having a copy of this new work to hand. The authors, both experienced lawyers, who also often speak at seminars and conferences for the housing and property industry and those professionals who are involved in it, have written a clear and thorough, and above all practical guide to this challenging area of law and practice. Readers will also find some ingenious suggestions about how to use the principles and the procedures to their advantage.

David Smith and Francis Davy are to be congratulated for having found the time to produce such a helpful guide.

Professor James Driscoll

LLM, LLB, Solicitor

Trowers & Hamlins

Tower Hill, London EC3N 4DX

List of Acts and Statutory Instruments

The following acts and statutory instruments are referenced in this publication.

Part 1: The Housing Health and Safety Rating System

Primary

> *Housing Act* 2004 ss 1–54; Schs 1–3

Secondary

> *The Housing Health and Safety Rating System (England) Regulations* 2005 (SI 2005/3208)

> *The Housing Health and Safety Rating System (Wales) Regulations* 2006 (SI 2006/1702 (W 164))

Part 2: Houses in Multiple Occupation and Licensing

Primary

> *Housing Act* 2004 ss 63–68; Schs 4, 5 and 14

Secondary

> *Town and Country Planning (Use Classes) Order* 1987 (SI 1987/764)

> *Selective Licensing of Houses (Specified Exemptions) (England) Order* 2006 (SI 2006/370)

> *Licensing of Houses in Multiple Occupation (Prescribed Descriptions) (England) Order* 2006 (SI 2006/371)

> *Management of Houses in Multiple Occupation (England) Regulations* 2006 (SI 2006/372)

> *Licensing and Management of Houses in Multiple Occupation and Other Houses (Miscellaneous Provisions) (England) Regulations* 2006 (SI 2006/373)

> *Houses in Multiple Occupation (Specified Educational Establishments) (England) Regulations* 2006 (SI 2006/647)

Housing Act 2004 (Commencement No. 5 and Transitional Provisions and Savings)(England) Order 2006 (SI 2006/1060)

Housing Act 2004 (Commencement No. 3 and Transitional Provisions and Savings) (Wales) Order 2006 (SI 2006/1535 (W. 152))

Houses in Multiple Occupation (Specified Educational Establishments) (Wales) Regulations 2006 (SI 2006/1707 (W.169))

Licensing of Houses in Multiple Occupation (Prescribed Descriptions) (Wales) Order 2006 (SI 2006/1712 (W.174))

Management of Houses in Multiple Occupation (Wales) Regulations 2006 (SI 2006/1713 (W.175))

Licensing and Management of Houses in Multiple Occupation and Other Houses (Miscellaneous Provisions) (Wales) Regulations 2006 (SI 2006/1715 (W.177))

Houses in Multiple Occupation (Specified Educational Establishments) (England) (No. 2) Regulations 2006 (SI 2006/2280)

Selective Licensing of Houses (Specified Exemptions) (Wales) Order 2006 (SI 2006/2824 (W.247))

Selective Licensing of Houses (Additional Conditions) (Wales) Order 2006 (SI 2006/2825 (W.248))

Licensing and Management of Houses in Multiple Occupation (Additional Provisions) (England) Regulations 2007 (SI 2007/1903)

Houses in Multiple Occupation (Certain Converted Blocks of Flats) (Modifications to the Housing Act 2004 and Transitional Provisions for section 257 HMOs) (England) Regulations 2007 (SI 2007/1904)

Licensing and Management of Houses in Multiple Occupation (Additional Provisions) (Wales) Regulations 2007 (SI 2007/3229 (W.281))

Houses in Multiple Occupation (Certain Blocks of Flats) (Modifications to the Housing Act 2004 and Transitional Provisions for section 257 HMOs) (Wales) Regulations 2007 (SI 2007/3231 (W.283))

Part 3: Control Provisions

Primary

Housing Act 2004 ss. 101–147 and Schs 6–7

Secondary

Housing (Empty Dwelling Management Orders) (Prescribed Exceptions and Requirements) (England) Order 2006 (SI 2006/367)

Housing (Management Orders and Empty Dwelling Management Orders) (Supplemental Provisions) (England) Regulations 2006 (SI 2006/368)

Housing (Empty Dwelling Management Orders) (Prescribed Exceptions and Requirements) (Wales) Order 2006 (SI 2006/2823 (W.246))

Housing (Management Orders and Empty Dwelling Management Orders) (Supplemental Provisions) (Wales) Regulations 2006 (SI 2006/2822 (W.245))

Housing (Interim Management Orders) (Prescribed Circumstances) (England) Order 2006 (SI 2006/369)

Housing (Interim Management Orders) (Prescribed Circumstances) (Wales) Order 2006 (SI 2006/1706 (W.168))

Part 4: Tenancy Deposit Protection
Primary

Housing Act 2004 ss 212–215 and Sch. 10

Secondary

Housing (Tenancy Deposit Schemes) Order 2007 (SI 2007/796)

Housing (Tenancy Deposits) (Prescribed Information) Order 2007 (SI 2007/797)

Housing (Tenancy Deposits) (Specified Interest Rate) Order 2007 (SI 2007/798)

Housing Act 2004 (Commencement No 7) (England) Order 2007 (SI 2007/1068)

Housing Act 2004 (Commencement No 4) (Wales) Order 2007 (SI 2007/305 (W 24))

Part 5: The Residential Property Tribunal
Primary

Housing Act 2004 ss. 230–231 and Sch. 13

Secondary

Residential Property Tribunal Procedure (England) Regulations 2006 (SI 2006/831)

Residential Property Tribunal (Fees) (England) Regulations 2006 (SI 2006/830)

Residential Property Tribunal Procedure (Wales) Regulations 2006 (SI 2006/1641)

Residential Property Tribunal (Fees) (Wales) Regulations 2006 (SI 2006/1642)

Table of cases

Residential Property Tribunal

Magistrates' Court

High Court

Court of Appeal and House of Lords

Introduction

The vast bulk of this book about the *Housing Act* 2004 is of direct concern to those managing residential property in the private sector. The authors have not touched on the rather miscellaneous collection of provisions to be found at the end of the Act which are of interest to social landlords (such as those touching on secure tenancies and the right to buy), to conveyancers (home information packs), or to rather specialist concerns (for example, mobile homes).

The changes to the legislative regime made by the *Housing Act* 2004 are considerable. Part 1 – the Housing Health and Safety Rating System – is a revolutionary new system for controlling "hazards" in residential property. It replaces a rather rigid system of "fitness" that existed under the *Housing Act* 1985 and has a very much wider scope.

Part 2 reforms the law on houses in multiple occupation (HMOs). It creates a new (and complex) definition of what is an HMO, which also attempts, rather unsuccessfully in the authors' view, to integrate the law on converted blocks of flats.

Part 3 permits local authorities to require licensing of non-HMO residential lettings in certain circumstances. Taken together, Parts 2 and 3 will bring large numbers of residential lettings into the ambit of local authority licensing. One manager of a major letting agency rather gloomily opined to the authors that, in his view, mandatory licensing of all residential lettings was only a matter of time, and that Parts 2 and 3 paved the way.

Part 4 of the Act deals with the power of local authorities to take over badly managed residential lettings or to take over and let empty dwellings. Again, the local authorities' powers are changed in fundamental ways from those that existed in the past.

All these new or reformed powers exercised by the local authorities will be policed in the greater part by a new judicial body: the residential property tribunal (RPT). The RPT is operated (in England) by the Residential Property Tribunal Service, which many readers will already know as the organisation that operates leasehold valuation tribunals and rent assessment committees. All three bodies draw their personnel from a group of lawyers, surveyors and other property practitioners known as Rent Assessment Panels. A similar sharing of personnel and management exists in Wales.

This book has proved far harder to write than the authors anticipated. At first blush the *Housing Act* 2004 is just another piece of legislation. It imposes significant obligations, to be sure, but the concepts of protecting tenancy deposits or of licensing properties would not appear to hold any great difficulty. Unfortunately that is not the case. For a number of reasons, many of which remain unclear, the Act is not only a complicated and in some cases rather tortuous piece of legislation, it has also spawned over 14 commencement orders in England and Wales, and another 20 or so pieces of secondary legislation which clarify, or alter, its operation. As if that were not bad enough, large areas of the law (such as the HHSRS) rely on extra-statutory documents for their operation. When these are added in, the Act rapidly becomes a huge document with large numbers of competing concepts to understand and many cross-references to be followed.

This book is intended primarily as a practical rather than theoretical guide. While the authors believe that the law is well covered and not misstated, for those readers looking for a more comprehensive statement of the law, the authors would recommend Professor James Driscoll's *Housing: The New Law: A Practical Guide to the Housing Act 2004.*

The Act has travelled a long road. As this book goes to press in early 2008, the last parts of the Act are only now coming into force, some four years after the Bill was introduced. It should be clear from this text that there are still a number of areas of uncertainty in the operation of the Act which will have to be decided by the courts or will need to be clarified by further legislation, or both.

This book is divided roughly along the lines that the Act itself follows, with each part of the book corresponding to a Part of the Act. It therefore has separate sections dealing with houses in multiple occupation, tenancy deposit protection, the housing health and safety rating system, management and control orders, and the residential property tribunals. This is by no means the only possible way of dividing up the text, and many of the topics cross-cut each other. We have tried to highlight situations where this will occur and provide cross-references, but it should always be borne in mind that the Act is intended to operate in an integrated manner and that any division of it is largely artificial. That said, we hope that the structure of the book will allow individuals to look at a chapter that deals with their immediate problem and gain most of the information they need on the spot. Each Part begins by setting out the primary legislation and secondary legislation that speaks to that particular area. Within the chapters there are references to legislation, guidance, and decisions of the RPT, where appropriate.

Although the authors have cited many decisions of the RPT, these are meant to be illustrative, and should be treated with caution. The RPT is not bound by its own decisions or those of its precursor organisations. While most recent decisions of the RPT have shown great respect for previous decisions, to the extent of explaining when a tribunal seems to depart from a previous decision, there is no necessity in law for them to do so. The experience of the RAC and LVT is that such an approach cannot be relied on in general.

The chapters stand on their own in the first instance. At the early stages of a problem each chapter should give sufficient information to explain the issues concerned, and how best to respond. They should also give an idea of where to dig to seek more information. For those dealing with the tribunals, we would advise a brief reading of the chapter on tribunal procedure first, and then a reading of the chapter that deals with the specific area that is of concern before a return to the tribunal chapter to formulate a detailed plan of action.

The book also operates as a portal by flagging up where it has sourced its information, and from it aims to serve as a starting point into issues surrounding the Act. It will answer many questions by itself, but it should also point to where further information can be sought. This book also, quite intentionally, seeks to subvert the Act. It highlights loopholes and problems whenever possible and shows how canny landlords and tenants or their advisors might seek to bend the legislation to their will. Naturally, this is always a risky pastime.

Part 1

The Housing Health and Safety Rating System

1

The Housing Health and Safety Rating System

Introduction

The Housing Health and Safety Rating System (or HHSRS for short) was introduced by Part I of the *Housing Act* 2004. It was commenced on 6 April 2006 along with other provisions of the *Housing Act* 2004 relating to licensing of HMOs and other rental properties. Further details of the operation are laid out in SI 2005/3208 and SI 2006/1702 in Wales (The '*HHSRS Regulations*'). Arguably, the HHSRS represents one of the most significant and far-reaching parts of the *Housing Act* 2004, from the point of view of residential lettings. It sets wide-ranging criteria under which local authorities are able to inspect rented accommodation, and couples this with substantial enforcement powers.

This chapter seeks to provide a guide to the key parts of the HHSRS and an indication of where further information can be found, as well as highlighting areas where local authorities are exceeding their powers or failing to fulfil their responsibilities, and the manner in which they have been successfully challenged.

While the *HHSRS Regulations* loosely set out the method by which the system should operate, the detail has been left entirely to a series of guidance documents published by the CLG department and available on their website at www.communities.gov.uk.

There are two guidance documents available: the *Operating Guidance* and the *Enforcement Guidance*. There is a further advisory document which is intended to summarise the two primary documents for the benefit of landlords and their agents. All the documents are extremely long and dense (even the summary) but, regrettably, an understanding of them is

7

vital if any realistic attempt is to be made to challenge a local authority decision. The difficulty of comprehending these documents has led to the publication by Asset Skills (see www.assetskills.org) of a landlord's guide to the HHSRS, which can be found on their website.

This chapter cannot hope to recreate the information found in the *Operating* and *Enforcement Guidance*, but does aim to summarise the method by which the system operates, and to sketch out possibilities by which any enforcement process initiated by the local authority can be challenged. Wherever possible, we have sought to give references to the *Operating* and *Enforcement Guidance* to allow interested individuals to seek further information.

Background

The HHSRS is designed to entirely replace the previous system of repairing notices under the *Housing Act* 1985. In fact it replaces not only the system of notices itself, but also the entire way of thinking associated with notices. This radical change has led to a full retraining of Environmental Health Officers (EHOs), and it is the severity of the challenges faced by them and other practitioners in the field which has made the task of getting to grips with the HHSRS so demanding. Previously, EHOs assessed properties largely by looking for items that were defective or non-functional, and then demanding that these things were fixed. This system, while effective, was limited in scope and was also highly prescriptive. It could often have the appearance of being a 'sledgehammer to crack a nut', causing annoyance to landlords served with apparently draconian notices over minor issues, while simultaneously frustrating EHOs by not allowing them to deal with things that should have been present in a property and weren't (such as adequate heating!). The HHSRS is intended to provide a more proportionate system focused on the impact of problems on the lives of the occupiers of a property.

As the HHSRS *Operating Guidance* states, the

> 'HHSRS is evidence-based. It is supported by extensive reviews of the literature and by detailed analyses of statistical data on the impact of housing conditions on health' (para. 1.04).

The HHSRS is based on evidence derived from studies relating to housing health, as well as on detailed analysis of accident statistics. It aims to use statistical data to give an objective and repeatable result, but one which is proportionate and takes account of the individual property being assessed. However, this does not appear to have been achieved.

In their report on local authority work with the private rented sector, the Chartered Institute for Housing (CIH) highlighted comments made by local authority staff in which they repeatedly stated that scores for the same property could vary widely between inspectors (see the interactive version of this at www.waysandmeans.idea.gov.uk). They also highlighted that it took much longer to survey properties under the HHSRS than under the previous regime, thereby increasing workload significantly.

The nature of the evidence has also been called into question. Most of the evidence comes from large-scale statistical studies of the entire housing population, such as the English House Condition Survey (EHCS), and there is doubt as to whether such a mass survey can be realistically applied to the state of an individual property. The statistical evidence is also somewhat out-of-date and is unlikely to be brought back into date. To use the example of the EHCS again, the HHSRS was largely based on the EHCS report from 1996, and has had little new data fed in from more recent surveys.

Overview

A residential property is inspected. Individual 'hazards' are identified and then a hazard score is generated for each hazard, based on the likelihood of an occurrence resulting from that hazard and the level of harm that could result from that occurrence.

This two-stage approach is intended to be more logical and to allow comparison between likely hazards with minor consequences and unlikely hazards with serious consequences (*Operating Guidance* para. 3.03). This should mean that each hazard is judged on its individual merits, rather than applying a catch-all approach. However, there is a view among some EHOs that the HHSRS is biased towards safety, and that health is a poor cousin.

Example

A property has a large, easily-opened, window with a low sill. A small child could climb onto the sill and open the window relatively easily and could then fall out through the open window. If that window is on the ground floor and there is grass beneath it, the danger from such a fall is minor and the most likely result is bruising. Such a window will attract a relatively low hazard score. However, if that same window is on the third floor and there is asphalt or, worse, a spiked railing, beneath it, then the outcome of a fall would be very severe and the hazard score will be correspondingly higher.

The aim of the HHSRS is to ensure that all premises provide a safe and healthy environment with adequate protection against local environmental hazards. Therefore the needs of a property in London (for security and noise protection, for example) might well differ from one in the Lake District, and this should be reflected in the scoring for each property. There is always a need to trade off the risks of any feature of the premises with the benefits provided by that feature, and this is recognised by the *Operating Guidance*.

Example

Fitting window locks to a property will reduce the risk of intruders. However, fitting such locks might increase the difficulty in exiting the property in the event of a fire. Depending on the location of the property and the balance between fire risk and security needs in the local area, the fitting of window locks may be required. So an EHO in a city with a high crime rate may require the fitting of window locks, as he will consider this the most pressing issue, while an EHO in a rural area with low crime may be uninterested in the ability to lock windows.

The Average

The standard is based on the average property as measured by the EHCS, which is a surprisingly high standard to set. This highlights the fact that the HHSRS seeks to improve the quality of residential properties and, as such, is aspirational in scope. EHOs will try to make properties better than they are, and local authorities are expected to raise the bar over time.

The Hazard Profiles

There are 29 hazard profiles under which a property can be assessed. These are divided into the following four groups:

1 Physiological requirements.
2 Psychological requirements.

3   Protection against infection.
4   Protection against accidents.

As will be clear in the discussion of the assessment process, when assessing a hazard, the inspector is not interested in how the property is currently being used, and will apply an objective standard of assessment. This standard is based on the potential users of the property who are believed to be at greatest risk from the hazard, and is usually expressed by reference to vulnerable age groups. Table 1 below sets out the 29 hazards, along with a brief description where appropriate, along with the groups used to assess the hazard.

Table 1 Hazard profiles

	Hazard	Comments
A	**PHYSIOLOGICAL REQUIREMENTS**	
	Hygrothermal conditions	
1	Damp and mould growth	This is often linked with the Excess Cold profile.
2	Excess cold	See below.
3	Excess heat	See below.
	Pollutants (non-microbial)	
4	Asbestos (and MMF)	Seen by the HHSRS as increasingly unimportant in the UK. Note that asbestos itself is not forbidden; it must be in a safe condition, and ideally clad in some manner.
5	Biocides	See below.
6	Carbon monoxide and fuel combustion products	This is usually associated with poorly fitted or maintained heating systems and will often be accompanied by a failure under hazard 9 or a breach of the *Gas Safety (Installation and Use) Regulations* 1988.
7	Lead	Usually from water pipes.
8	Radiation	Usually from radon, a highly localised problem in the UK.
9	Uncombusted fuel gas	See hazard 6.
10	Volatile organic compounds	See below.

B PSYCHOLOGICAL REQUIREMENTS

Space, security, light and noise

11	Crowding and space	This hazard should only be considered from the point of view of the current occupants. See *Enforcement Guidance* para. 4.23.
12	Entry by intruders	No vulnerable group. The surrounding area and its design are relevant factors when considering the level of security required on the dwelling. As has already been discussed, a balance needs to be struck between protection and fire safety and mental health. However, window locks, standard of repair, basic external lighting, spy holes and door furniture will all be seen as fairly minimum requirements.
13	Lighting	There must be adequate natural light for health purposes and sufficient artificial light to prevent eye strain. Sighting of lights and controls is important to allow for ease of use. See *Enforcement Guidance* paras 13.06–13.14.
14	Noise	This is an issue which causes high levels of complaint and is one that EHOs are under pressure to address. Good construction is a key component of noise reduction, but in high noise areas extra measures including double or triple glazing, and additional noise insulation may be needed.

C PROTECTION AGAINST INFECTION

Hygiene, sanitation and water supply

15	Domestic hygiene, pests and refuse	No vulnerable group. This profile is mainly an issue of good repair.
16	Food safety	Adequate food storage, preparation areas, sinks with drainers and hot and cold running water, and sufficient plug sockets will be a minimum standard. Damp will be a major negative factor. In HMOs, sufficient food storage and preparation space to allow separation between households will be necessary.

17	Personal hygiene, sanitation and drainage	This should be largely self-explanatory. The main cause of problems will be disrepair and insufficient facilities for the number of occupants.
18	Water supply	For mains supplied systems this should not be an issue. Problems will likely occur where storage tanks on site are insufficiently covered or made from unsuitable material and therefore permitting water contamination.

D PROTECTION AGAINST ACCIDENTS

Falls

19	Falls associated with baths etc	This profile is most concerned with individuals over 60, due to the severe health effects of slips at that age. It is most concerned with appropriate slip resistance in baths, showers and other wet areas. However, appropriate ergonomics in positioning of taps and other controls will also be relevant.
20	Falling on level surfaces etc	Issues such as tread, evenness, lighting, ambient temperature and state of repair will all be crucial in determining likelihood of occurrence. For outdoor surfaces, drainage may also be important. The nature of the surface will also determine variation in the injury likelihood.
21	Falling on stairs etc	This constitutes one of the most critical hazards under the HHSRS, with some of the highest chances of the most critical harms. Particularly steep stairs and those which are open or without handrails will attract higher scores. Carpeted stairs will reduce scores and risk of injury. Remember that this hazard will include a consideration of all stairs associated with the dwelling, including external stairs, and the score will be adjusted depending on the frequency of use.

| 22 | Falling between levels | This hazard is based on falls from balconies and windows but is only relevant where the drop between the levels is in excess of 300mm. It is calculated on the basis of a child under five years old. This profile is important as this type of fall represents one of the most common causes of death in children. Ease of opening windows and the amount by which they can be opened will be important. Ease of cleaning will also have an effect on the score. Unsurprisingly, the fall height and nature of the ground underneath will be crucial factors in determining the injury scores. Window restrictors and adequate balcony railings (at least 1100mm high and weight-bearing) will be necessary, although restrictors should be able to be overridden to avoid conflicting with the fire profile (see below). |

Electric shocks, fires, burns and scalds

23	Electrical hazards	While these do not often rate high scores, the ease by which this hazard can be assessed can cause disproportionate enforcement. Many EHOs will rely on reports from electricians who will assess the electrical installation on the basis of current standards.
24	Fire	See below.
25	Flames, hot surfaces etc	Hot surfaces against which individuals may become trapped should be covered such that the temperature is below 43°C. Bath tap temperature should be limited to 44–46°C, while sinks should be limited to 60°C.

Collisions, cuts and strains

| 26 | Collision and entrapment | Issues under this profile are due to poor design and placement of doors and windows so that they project over walkways or open inappropriately. Note that safety glazing will be required in accordance with Part N of the *Building Regulations*. |
| 27 | Explosions | This profile should not be a cause for concern but is usually linked to hazards 6 and 9 and will be concerned with failures to obtain appropriate gas safety certifications. |

| 28 | Position and operability of amenities etc | This profile is of minimal importance as the harm caused is low. It is concerned primarily with ease of operation of facilities. |
| 29 | Structural collapse and falling elements | In properly constructed and properly maintained dwellings this profile should be irrelevant. |

A detailed discussion of all the hazard profiles is not appropriate to this text and the reader is referred to the *Operating Guidance*. However, it may be useful to discuss some of the more important and unusual profiles.

Excess cold

This is a very important profile. The CIH pointed out that there are a large number of properties that are achieving high scores in this hazard profile. The *Operating Guidance* states that there are 40,000 more deaths than would be expected between December and March every year in the UK. Inadequately heated property is a significant contributory factor to this. EHOs therefore take this hazard extremely seriously and will act decisively where it is identified.

The *Operating Guidance* sets a high standard, requiring heating systems to be able to maintain a temperature of 21°C in living areas when the external temperature is 5°C. Anecdotal evidence suggests that some EHOs appear to have gone beyond this, requiring the higher standard of an internal temperature of 21°C when the external temperature is -1°C. It is questionable whether this is permissible, and such determinations could form the basis of an appeal.

It is also worth noting that the required actions set by EHOs usually include the installation, or radical improvement, of a central heating system. This is a very expensive business and landlords should either pre-empt this by installing cheaper, but nevertheless effective, heating systems such as night-storage heaters, or should seek to negotiate with the local authority at an early stage to agree a more cost effective solution to the problem.

Recall that the objective is to improve properties to the average, and the average in England for properties is quite high when it comes to heating and insulation. Over 80% of dwellings have gas-fired central heating and over 70% have more than 100mm of loft insulation. Over 85% of dwellings have partial or full double glazing. Therefore, landlords can expect EHOs to set high standards in respect of heating and insulation, and they will have the data to support such contentions.

The excess cold statistic remains problematic as the guidance places a very high emphasis on it. The statistics it relies on, quoted above, are debatable. Excess winter deaths cannot entirely be attributed to cold homes and are also caused by disease, increased accidents in conditions of poor light and slippery surfaces, and other incidents. The use of these statistics provides a highly distorted picture and the hazard rating for excess cold that results has led to concern that EHOs will be sidetracked into costly and time-consuming enforcement action for relatively small improvements in property. The growth of Energy Performance Certificates and their expected introduction into let property from October 2008 will, no doubt, continue to feed into this area.

Excess heat

This may seem to be a slightly unusual profile, given the prevailing view of the British climate. However, medical professionals have identified excess deaths among the elderly and very young during heatwaves, and poorly ventilated property is a clear contributory factor to this. Thus far this profile seems to be used largely to ensure that landlords deal with windows that have been painted shut and other such matters of poor ventilation, but it would not take a great leap of imagination to see enthusiastic EHOs demanding air conditioning units or coolers being installed into properties where there was a significant problem.

Protection from intruders

While many landlords will already fulfil this requirement due to insurance prescriptions, there remains a significant proportion of properties that will be required to improve security arrangements by fitting window locks and improving the quality of door locks so that they comply with the basic security requirement of a five-lever lock with deadlock capability along with a supplementary five-lever deadlock. Note that in order to satisfy the fire safety profile, any such lock must be capable of being opened from inside without a key, by the use of a thumb turn or similar. Many EHOs also consider security lighting in appropriate locations to be a key component of this requirement and will increase their demands where properties are not easily visible to casual passers by.

Fire safety

This profile is very important and has the potential to affect the majority of rented property in England and Wales. Unsurprisingly, EHOs take this matter very seriously. The problem lies with the standards being used to assess fire safety. The HHSRS supplies very limited guidance on this point and therefore most EHOs have adopted the standards set out in the guidance for sleeping accommodation produced to supplement the *Regulatory Reform (Fire Safety) Order* 2005. This guidance is available at www.firesafetylaw.communities.gov.uk. This position has been confirmed by a new voluntary protocol to ensure cooperation between local authorities and fire services, which can be found at www.lacors.gov.uk/lacors/ContentDetails.aspx?id=16453. Without going into detail, the kind of standards within the guidance which are being sought by EHOs include:

- fire blankets and fire extinguishers in kitchens;
- half-hour fireproofing on all doors;
- automatic closing systems on all doors;
- interlinked, mains-powered smoke alarms with battery back-up.

Many older properties, particularly those which involve houses converted into flats, will not meet these standards and may require significant alteration. It is particularly worth noting that properties in which it is necessary to pass through a kitchen, especially an open-plan kitchen, in order to exit the premises are a particular bugbear for many EHOs, and will usually require substantial work. Many EHOs will take advice from local fire authorities and their recommendations and their views appear to be persuasive in the case of an appeal (LON/00AY/HIN/2006/2001).

Biocides

This category covers threats to health from those chemicals used to treat timber and mould growth in dwellings. While biocides include insecticides and rodenticides to control pest infestations (e.g. cockroaches or rats and mice), these are not considered for the purposes of the HHSRS. This problem would most commonly be found where industrial products have been used in an inappropriate manner.

Volatile organic compounds

Volatile organic compounds (VOCs) are a diverse group of organic chemicals such as formaldehyde, that are gaseous at room temperature and are found in a wide variety of materials in the home. These should not normally cause a problem unless chemicals have been used in an inappropriate manner. It may be an issue in properties built on landfill or other previously contaminated ground where insufficient steps have been taken to deal with contaminants leaching from the ground.

Radiation

This is a geographically highly limited hazard as it refers primarily to contamination by radon gas. The authors have assumed that other forms of radioactive hazard are not normally found in residential homes! Therefore this issue should be largely confined to Cornwall and other areas where radon seepage is an issue and should be easily dealt with through adequate ventilation.

Inspection regime

The HHSRS only applies to residential premises in the private sector. It does not apply to local authority stock. Any form of accommodation used for human habitation is classed as a dwelling so long as it is a building or a part of a building – so that mobile homes are not liable to inspection. The definition of a dwelling includes paths, yards, gardens and outbuildings associated with the dwelling as well as any rights, easements or services necessary to live there. It is irrelevant whether these are shared (*Operating Guidance* paras 2.05–2.06).

It is also irrelevant that the dwelling concerned may be empty, since inspection is based on a notional occupier. It is not therefore relevant that there is an intention on the part of the landlord to evict the current occupiers and then reconstruct the property, and this is not a reason for a local authority not to inspect or to require improvements (MAN/00BN/HIN/2006/0009).

Where an application has been made for a premises licence in accordance with Parts II or III of the *Housing Act* 2004, an HHSRS inspection must be made within five years of the application, although the grant of a licence should not be delayed pending such an inspection. The authority is obliged to inspect where they consider 'that it would be appropriate' for a property to be inspected (s. 4(1)). Local authorities are also required to carry out an inspection where a formal written complaint is made by a justice of the peace with jurisdiction over the area concerned, or by a parish or community council within the district.

The authority has no direct obligation to inspect where a complaint by the occupier is made, and some EHOs have proved reluctant to do so. One option to force the issue may be to get a local parish council interested, particularly in rural areas. Where this is not an option and EHOs are not taking action, then tenants or their advisors might wish to point out that paragraph 2.6 of the *Enforcement Guidance* states: 'While there is not an express duty on local authorities to inspect properties where they think there might be hazards, sections 3 and 4 of the Act, when taken together, imply that an authority should have good reason not to investigate further.' There is therefore a good case in these circumstances for asking the local authority to explain on what basis they are declining to inspect. Not wanting to get involved is certainly insufficient.

The local authority might also be reminded that it is the guiding principle of the HHSRS that 'Any residential premises should provide a safe and healthy environment for any potential occupier or visitor' (*Operating Guidance* para. 1.12). The authors have found such an argument, possibly coupled with a letter under the Judicial Review pre-action protocol, persuasive when EHOs are reluctant to take action.

The Notional Occupier

The concept of a notional occupier is vital to the HHSRS. The hazard score is not calculated on the basis of any current occupier of a property, but is always based on a theoretical occupier who will be assumed to be from the most vulnerable groups in society. Where a hazard profile requires a vulnerable group to be specified, it normally aims for children under the age of five or adults over 65. This means that when thinking about hazards it is vital to think of them from the point of view of these groups. A flight of stairs for example should not be considered from the point of view of a young healthy adult but rather from the perspective of an elderly person.

Interestingly, the definition of property subject to inspection also includes property let on long leaseholds or occupied by an owner-occupier. It is perfectly possible, although exceptional, for an owner-occupier to be served with a notice or order requiring them to repair their own property, and such orders have been made and confirmed on appeal (see BIR/17UB/HPO/2006/0002).

While the HHSRS legislation and guidance has set out procedures to be followed to ensure that it does not fall foul of the right to a fair trial guaranteed by Article 6 of the *European Convention on Human Rights*, it is more questionable whether the serving of a Prohibition Order on an owner-occupier would breach the right to respect for private and family life guaranteed by Article 8. However, given the House of Lords decisions in *Lambeth LBC v Kay*and *Leeds CC v Price* [2006] HLR 22, where it was made clear that the correct operation of a statutory provision will normally provide the necessary justification for a breach of Article 8, it seems unlikely that such a case could be sustained. As the HHSRS uses a notional concept of the most vulnerable occupant, empty property is also capable of being assessed. However, local authorities should consider what the intended use of the property is in the near future, and tailor their enforcement action accordingly (*Enforcement Guidance para. 4.20*). There is little point in serving a Prohibition Order on an empty property that the landlord intends to substantially reconstruct, for example.

Scoring

The hazard score is calculated by multiplying the probability of an event within the next 12 months by the scale of harm that will be caused by that event happening. This produces a score ranging from 0 to 1 million. This score is transformed into a hazard band from A to J, according to Table 2 below.

Table 2 Hazard band scoring

Band	Hazard Score Range	Band	Hazard Score Range
A	5,000 or more	F	100 to 199
B	2,000 to 4,999	G	50 to 99
C	1,000 to 1,999	H	20 to 49
D	500 to 999	I	10 to 19
E	200 to 499	J	9 or less

Once the hazard band has been found this is mutated into a hazard category. Hazards in band C or higher are category 1 hazards, hazards below band C are category 2 hazards. This means that any hazard with a score over 1000 will fall into category 1 while anything lower than this will be in category 2.

Harm

There are four classes of harm, ranging from extreme to moderate. Extreme harms are those which will cause death or severe and permanent disablement. Severe harms would cause significant disablement for a substantial time period or long-term disfigurement. Serious harms are those which would cause moderate disablement or serious or long-term inconvenience. Moderate harms would cause minor disablement or recurring illness. Examples of injuries that might fall into the various harm categories are set out in Sch. 2 to the *HHSRS Regulations* (see Table 3 below).

It should be noted that many harms that fall into the lowest two categories are hazards that would not normally be seen as issues, and under previous schemes would not have even been registered by Environmental Health Officers.

Table 3 Classification of types of harm

Class of harm	Types of harm
I Extreme	Death, lung cancer, permanent paralysis, 80% burns
II Severe	Asthma, lead poisoning, mild stroke, loss of hand or foot, serious fractures, serious burns
III Serious	Diarrhoea, vomiting, mild heart attack, sick building syndrome, loss of a finger, severe concussion
IV Moderate	Benign tumours, broken finger, moderate cuts, severe bruising, slight concussion, regular severe coughs or colds

The majority of hazards, particularly the more esoteric ones, have very low likelihoods of occurrence and fairly low harm statistics and therefore they are not likely to result in any repairing obligation accruing to the landlord. Given the relative safety and exhaustive testing requirements associated with modern building materials, hazards such as asbestos and biocides are now extremely rare. The most serious hazards, as might be expected, are those within the Protection Against Accidents group and, particularly, falls. It is also worth noting that the HHSRS does consider 'social' factors such as sufficient space and appropriate security, and while this is outside the experience of many Environmental Health Officers, they have taken this on board and will act to ensure that these hazards are taken seriously by landlords.

Calculation

The calculation formula is quite complex. EHOs have the benefit of handheld computers to do the calculations, but the rest of us must make do with consulting the relevant tables in the *Operating Guidance* and use a calculator!

Each hazard profile has an associated table in the *Operating Guidance* giving a guide to the statistical calculations required. The table for the profile associated with falls down stairs is reproduced in Table 4 below.

Table 4 Hazard profile – falling on stairs

Falling on stairs Average likelihood and health outcomes for all persons aged 60 years and over, 1997–1999							
Dwelling Type and Age		Average Likeli- hood I in %	**Spread of Health Outcomes**				Average HHSRS Scores
			Class I %	Class 2 %	Class 3 %	Class 4 %	
Houses	Pre-1920	218	2.2	7.7	22.1	68.0	170 (F)
	1920–1945	226	2.1	7.4	20.5	80.0	156 (F)
	1946–1979	226	1.6	6.6	21.6	70.2	116 (F)
	Post-1979	256	1.4	6.3	25.3	67.0	112 (F)
Flats	Pre-1920	214	3.9	8.0	19.3	68.8	249 (E)
	1920–1945	263	1.6	2.8	20.1	75.5	97 (G)
	1946–1979	410	2.8	5.3	17.7	74.2	96 (G)
	Post-1979	409	2.6	5.2	21.4	72.8	92 (G)
	All	**245**	**1.9**	**6.7**	**19.7**	**69.7**	**134 (F)**

As can be seen from the table, the EHO enters with the approximate age of the property and the table then gives an average likelihood for an occurrence of this hazard. The EHO then decides, on the basis of his or her knowledge and experience, whether the likelihood should be altered. So, for example a staircase without a banister or with poorly secured carpeting will probably have the likelihood of an accident on it adjusted upwards significantly. It should be noted that the likelihood can be adjusted where properties are shared among multiple individuals. It is this question of probability of accident which allows EHOs the greatest scope for adjustment to the overall score. A relatively small adjustment in probability can lead to a large change in the overall score.

Case study

In one case an EHO amended the probability of excess cold from 1 in 330 to 1 in 56, as he deemed the property to be particularly poor. This led to an overall hazard score in excess of 8,000.

Often such changes will be made without any particular rationale being provided. Different EHOs will also take a very different view of how much a particular hazard should have its probability adjusted. EHOs are often very reluctant to reveal how they have arrived at their probability scores.

The table also provides the EHO with a percentage score, indicating the percentage of incidents which cause injuries falling into each of the four categories of harm. Again, the inspector may choose to adjust this depending on local circumstances so, for example, a set of stairs with sharp metal edging will have the percentages relating to more severe injuries increased accordingly.

Example – a house with three sets of steps and stairs

- At the front gate there are two steps. These are of rough concrete and have high risers. There is a crude loose handrail to one side.
- At the front door there are four steps of smooth concrete. The bottom step is higher than the others. There is a steel tube handrail to one side.
- The internal stairs have two windows at the top. The stairs are fairly steep, but not more than the average for this type of dwelling (a 1930s detached house) and there is a handrail to one side.

There is nothing to suggest that the outcomes from a fall on the internal stairs will be anything other than average (i.e. 2.1%, 7.4%, 20.5% and 70.0% for Classes I, II, III, and IV respectively). However, the state and condition of the steps to the front door and those near the front gate, are such that it is judged that the Class I outcome to a person aged 60 years or more from a fall at either of these locations will be increased, particularly if that fall was in cold weather or at night. The representative scale points of the outcomes are judged to be 4.6%, 10.00%, 21.5% and 63.8% respectively.

Operating Guidance, para. 3.16

When the EHO has worked out all his figures he must then calculate a score for each of the categories of harm, taking into account the likelihood of an accident, the percentage chance of an injury in that category of harm occurring, and the multiplier for that harm category. So the calculation for each category looks like this:

$$\text{CatScore} = \frac{1}{\text{likelihood}} \times \text{harm} \times \text{multiplier}$$

Each class of harm has a multiplier associated with it which reflects its seriousness. These are set out in Table 5 below.

Table 5 Class of Harm multipliers

Class of harm	Multiplier
I Extreme	10,000
II Severe	1,000
III Serious	300
IV Moderate	10

Once a score has been calculated for the categories relating to the four classes of harm, these are added together to create an overall score for that particular hazard. The score is then transformed into a band and from there into one of the two categories of hazard as described above.

HMOs

EHOs can uplift scores, and particularly harm likelihoods, for HMO properties. However, EHOs continue to be frustrated that these assessments are made in relation to individual bedsits. This tends to ignore issues that relate to the HMO as a whole and makes them seem less important. EHOs may be tempted to compensate for this by making significant increases in likelihood scores for areas that they believe are not receiving sufficient attention.

Enforcement

As already stated, local authorities are compelled to take enforcement action with regard to Category 1 hazards and have a choice as to whether they should act in regard to Category 2 hazards. There is a requirement where any hazard is found for an EHO to make a written report 'without delay' to the local authority, which must consider the report 'as soon as possible' (s. 4(6) and (7)). The HHSRS gives a wide choice of enforcement options to local authorities, from mild rebukes through to full-fledged intervention.

The CIH discovered that the HHSRS requires authorities to intervene more often than was the case under the previous system of inspection. Anecdotal evidence suggests that most authorities concentrate their efforts on category 1 and the more serious of the category 2 hazards. However, a significant number of authorities will enforce category 2 hazards as well. Originally the government had intended that hazards lower than band G should have no formal enforcement action attached to them, but this idea was shelved and it was left to local authorities to decide their own priorities. However, anecdotal evidence shows that most local authorities do, in fact, have their own minimum level below which they will not take action.

Actions that can be taken

Hazard Awareness Notice

Improvement Notice
- Suspended Improvement Notice

Prohibition Order
- Suspended Prohibition Order
- Emergency Prohibition Order

Emergency remedial action

Demolition Order

Clearance Order

The HHSRS provides for several levels of enforcement of increasing severity. Informal action is preferred for dealing with Category 2 hazards, particularly where the landlord is inclined to be co-operative or the matter is of little importance. The majority of EHOs do seem to prefer this mode of action where possible and have largely done so by using letters modelled on the old 'minded to' letter seen under the Housing Act 1985 system. Local authorities are also required to consider the views of tenants, landlords and owners when formulating an enforcement policy (*Enforcement Guidance* para. 2.16) and the 'minded to' process seems to be the route by which many of them satisfy this requirement. Local authorities are always required to take the 'most appropriate [action] of those available to them' in each case (s. 5(4)).

- The Hazard Awareness Notice (HAN) is the lowest tier of formalised action and this should be used in most cases. However, the HAN has no direct power of enforcement associated with it and EHOs appear loath to use them for more serious issues.
- Improvement Notices set out a schedule of improvements that must be carried out to the property within a set time period. They are the lowest level of notice which has a direct criminal sanction associated with non-compliance.
- Prohibition Orders are a relatively severe sanction as they prohibit the use of the property or a part of it for specified purposes. They also have criminal sanctions associated with them. Where it is necessary to take urgent action in respect of a Category 1 hazard, a local authority may also use an Emergency Prohibition Order.
- Emergency remedial action. This enables local authorities to take urgent action themselves in serious cases where there is a risk to the health of the occupiers. This form of enforcement is not available for Category 2 hazards.
- Demolition and Clearance Orders have been retained in full from the *Housing Act* 1985 and offer a last resort power of action in serious cases. As with emergency remedial action, this form of enforcement is not available for Category 2 hazards.

The HHSRS *Enforcement Guidance* requires local authorities to take their local housing situations and strategy into account when deciding how to enforce the HHSRS:

> 'Authorities will need to take a view of the spread of hazards in the local housing stock that have come to their attention, and prioritise action on those with the most serious impact on health or safety. It might be an inappropriate diversion of resources and effort to deal with modest hazards when there is evidence of more serious hazards elsewhere.' (*Enforcement Guidance* para. 2.2)

They will be required to prioritise issues which are problems locally and to have a plan to deal effectively with these over time. Authorities have been encouraged to adopt the Enforcement Concordat (*Enforcement Guidance* para. 2.17) published by the Cabinet Office (see www.berr.gov.uk/bre) which requires them to give clear practical advice on how to resolve issues and to take the most appropriate and least onerous action appropriate to the circumstances. There is also a clear requirement on local authorities to act consistently when deciding how to take enforcement action (*Enforcement Guidance* para. 2.2).

Normally, a property which complies fully with current Building Regulations and the associated standards and Codes of Practice 'will usually achieve the Ideal for the majority of hazards as described in the operating guidance. In a few cases, the Ideal might be at a higher level than Building Regulations require. In practice, the difference will be negligible and is extremely unlikely to result in enforcement action' (*Enforcement Guidance* para. 4.18). If this is adhered to then modern properties or older properties converted or refurbished to modern standards should not find themselves sufficiently in contravention of the HHSRS standards to require formal enforcement action.

The RPT has stated that in some areas 'there is a point of divergence between the requirements of the Building Regulations and the HHSRS' and that in some cases 'compliance with the Building Regulations will [not] necessarily be sufficient to reduce the hazard to below Category 1' (MAN/32UB/HPO/2006/0004), and so there is potential for properties that are fully compliant with modern building methods and standards to fall foul of the HHSRS.

For Category 1 hazards the local authority is required to take formal action but, as stated above, they must take the most appropriate course of action available in the circumstances and they should only take one course of action at a time. This does not prevent the taking of an alternative course if the first one fails. In most circumstances EHOs are taking informal action first by sending a letter to the owner, modelled on the 'minded to' letter often used under the *Housing Act* 1985. Usually, this sets out the EHOs concerns and the hazards that have been found and indicates the action the EHO is intending to take. There is usually an opportunity for the person sent such a letter to respond before the EHO will take more formal action.

Minded-to letters

These are used where a hazard is not a severe risk and where the local authority wishes to offer an opportunity for matters to be put right. The advantage from the point of view of the person being sent such a letter is that, unlike a formal notice, they cannot be charged by the authority for the cost of sending such a letter. They are also an opportunity to negotiate with the authority at an early stage in the hope of avoiding further action. They should not be ignored, as the authority will usually set a time-limit by which they will take formal action and will, usually, stick to it if they do not hear anything. A robust but reasonable approach to such a letter will often see results.

Case study

A landlord was sent a minded-to letter stating that the local authority would serve an Improvement Notice in 28 days, for which they would charge over £300. To avoid this, they demanded that the landlord carry out improvements to electrical works and to the lighting in the property. The authority specifically wanted ceiling roses fitted in preference to uplighters, and portable lamps connected via special sockets to a wall switch. The landlord's legal advisors asked for further information from the local authority and questioned the basis of the requested improvements to the lighting. They assured the authority that the electrical works would be done but that the lighting changes would be contested. The parties settled on the basis that the electrical works would be done and that more lamps fitted with the appropriate plugs would be provided for the use of the tenants. This avoided the service of the Improvement Notice and the consequent charge.

Actions to take on the receipt of a minded-to letter

- Don't ignore it.
- Ask the authority to provide details of its calculations and how the likelihoods were arrived at.
- Look at the work the authority wants done. Consider its appropriateness and whether the same result can be achieved more economically or the hazard alleviated sufficiently to satisfy the requirement.
- Consider the potential to negotiate with the authority by doing some of the more important works and alleviating other issues.

Hazard Awareness Notices

Hopefully, the Hazard Awareness Notice (HAN) will be the normal form of enforcement action and should be used where the landlord has shown a willingness to cooperate. The HAN is specified by s. 28 for category 1 hazards and s. 29 for category 2 hazards. The required information for each is the same and is laid down by subss. (6) and (5) respectively. To satisfy the subsection an HAN must specify:

- the nature of the hazard and the residential premises on which it exists;
- the deficiency giving rise to the hazard;
- the premises on which the deficiency exists;
- the authority's reasons for deciding to serve the notice, including their reasons for deciding that serving the notice is the most appropriate course of action; and
- details of the remedial action (if any) which the authority consider that it would be practicable and appropriate to take in relation to the hazard.

The requirements of service are the same as those for Improvement Notices and are found in Schedule I Part I of the Act.

There are no powers of enforcement whatsoever attached to an HAN. In other words, the person on whom it is served is completely free to ignore it and nothing can be done directly. That said, if an HAN fails, then the local authority may, and probably will, choose to take more aggressive action.

Contents of Improvement Notices and Prohibition Orders

The required contents of Improvement Notices and Prohibition Orders are set out in ss. 12, 13, 22 and 23 of the Act, respectively. The two sections for each type of notice relate to whether the notice was served in relation to a category 1 or category 2 hazard. The requirements for the different forms of notice are, however, much the same. The notice must specify in relation to each hazard:

- which section the notice or order is being served under;
- the nature of the hazard and the residential premises on which it exists;
- the deficiency giving rise to the hazard;
- *for Improvement Notices,* the premises in relation to which remedial action is to be taken in respect of the hazard and the nature of that remedial action *or for Prohibition Orders* the premises in relation to which prohibitions are imposed by the order;

- *for Improvement Notices,* the date when the remedial action is to be started and the period within which the remedial action is to be completed or the periods within which each part of it is to be completed *or for Prohibition Orders* any remedial action which the authority consider would, if taken in relation to the hazard, result in their revoking the order.

The requirement to 'specify' the remedial action is vital and requires a 'definitive and directional statement with a degree of precision so that the recipient knows what he has to do to address the situation'. Thus a Prohibition Order was held to be invalid where the local authority had stated that the works needed for them to revoke the order were that the properties concerned be 'underpinned or ideally demolished and rebuilt off new foundations' as the statement was 'too vague and imprecise' (CAM/26UG/HPO/2006/0002). However, it appears that minor defects in a Prohibition Order will be tolerated as long as it is 'obvious to a reasonable occupant' what the Order is seeking to do.

Under s. 8 of the Act the local authority is required to prepare written reasons for the particular course of enforcement action and why this form of action was chosen over an alternative form. This statement is required to be served alongside Improvement Notices, Prohibition Orders, or Demolition Orders. As the *Enforcement Guidance* makes clear, this statement is required in order to satisfy concerns that the serving of such an order might breach the right to a fair hearing under Article 6 of the European Convention on Human Rights (*Enforcement Guidance* para. 4.7).

Tribunals have indicated that this statement must be served separately from the notice and must be explicit. It is unacceptable for a local authority to suggest that some other document, or the notice itself will satisfy this requirement (CAM/26UG/HPO/2006/0002). However, where such a statement has been made, however cursory, it appears to be seen as acceptable (CAM/00MB/HPO/2006/0001). The fact that no previous formal enforcement action has occurred or that the premises are unoccupied will not render the serving of a Prohibition Order (and by extension an Improvement Notice) disproportionate. It is also in order for the local authority to take into account the fact that remedial works will be expensive and that requiring such expenditure would be unreasonable and that the works required are unlikely to allow long-term occupation of the property (LON/00AL/HPO/2006/0001).

Key Things that must be stated in Improvement Notices and Prohibition Orders

- The nature of the hazard.
- What is causing the hazard.
- Where the hazard is.
- What section of the Act the Notice/Order is being served under.
- A **clear** explanation of what work needs to be done.
- Written reasons for choice of the method of enforcement.

Suspension of Notices and Orders

Section 14 of the Act confers the power on local authorities to suspend the operation of an Improvement Notice until a particular time or until the occurrence of a particular event as specified in the Order. A similar power is conferred in respect of Prohibition Orders by s. 23, with the added particularisation that the Order could be suspended until a particular person has left the property or until an undertaking has been breached. The RPTS has suggested that certain factors should be considered by a local authority when deciding whether to suspend an Order made due to an overcrowding hazard (CHI/00HB/HPO/2007/0005). However, the factors appear to have general applicability and therefore it would be reasonable to assume that any local authority should consider among other things:

- The seriousness of the hazard, and whether it is so serious as to require an Order to take effect immediately.
- The impact of an immediate Order on the occupants, taking into account:
  - how long the occupiers have occupied the premises whilst the hazard has existed;
  - whether the occupiers are members of a vulnerable group in so much as this has not already been considered in the hazard rating process;
  - the effect of the hazard on the occupiers' physical and mental health in so much as this has not already been considered in the hazard rating process;
  - the ages and genders of the occupants in so much as this has not already been considered in the hazard rating process;
  - any other relevant circumstances of the occupants.
- The state of repair of the premises.
- The likelihood of any of the occupants voluntarily vacating the premises and the availability of suitable alternative accommodation for them.

- The wishes of the occupants.
- Whether the decision to suspend the Order or not would result in a breach of Article 8 of the ECHR.

If the operation of a Notice or Order is suspended, then the local authority has the power to review it at any time and must do so not later than one year after the notice or order was served and at ongoing annual intervals. On review, the local authority must serve a copy of its decision in line with the service of the original Notice or Order.

The suspension of a Prohibition Order can be appealed on the basis that although the power to suspend a possession order is contained within a separate provision of the Act (s. 23), this does not mean that the suspension of an order is separate from the order itself and is simply a part of a Prohibition Order which provides for its operation to be suspended. Therefore an appeal against the suspension of an order is an appeal against the order itself (CHI/00HB/HPO/2007/0005). By extension it would be reasonable to conclude that a suspended Improvement Notice can be appealed on a similar basis.

Revocation and variation of Orders

Local authorities must revoke Prohibition Orders if the hazard which they complain of in the Order no longer exists on the premises. They may also choose to revoke such an order if there are special circumstances or if they consider it appropriate. Local authorities also have the power to vary the terms of an Order on the application of any party on whom such an Order is required to be served, or at their own discretion. If a variation is made with the consent of all parties on whom such an order was required to be served, then it will come into force immediately, otherwise it will not come into force until the appropriate time for an appeal has passed (see Appendix H).

Emergency Prohibition Orders

For serious cases where a local authority believes that there is a category 1 hazard in a property and that it poses an 'imminent risk of serious harm to the health or safety of any occupiers' in the property or in other residential property, then they are empowered to make an Emergency Prohibition Order under s. 43. This Order is the same as a normal Prohibition Order but it comes into effect immediately. It must be served in the same manner as an ordinary Prohibition Order, with the caveat that copies must be served not within seven days but on the day or as soon as possible after the day on which the order comes into force. Such an order must contain the following information:

- the nature of the hazard and the residential premises on which it exists;
- the deficiency giving rise to the hazard;
- the premises in relation to which emergency remedial action has been or is to be taken;
- the power under which the action is to be taken;
- the date when the remedial action was or is to be started.

Offences

If a person served with an Improvement Notice does not start work by the date specified in the notice and complete it within the time period specified in the notice or lodge an appeal, they commit an offence (s. 30). If the appeal fails then the tribunal will set a new date and time period by which the works must be started and completed; failure to comply with these dates will then constitute an offence. If an appeal is lodged and then withdrawn, the start date on the notice is moved into the future by 21 days and the time period to complete the work will remain the same.

Using a property in contravention of a Prohibition Order, or permitting the premises to be used in contravention of such an order also constitutes an offence (s. 32).

In both cases the penalty for the offence is a fine at scale 5 on the standard scale (currently £5,000). In addition, continuing to contravene a Prohibition Order after conviction leads to a further fine of up to £20 per day or part day. It is a defence to a prosecution under a Notice or Order that it was reasonable to fail to comply with it.

Enforcement action on Improvement Notices

Local authorities are empowered to take action to do works themselves if works are not carried out in accordance with an Improvement Notice. This power is set out in Sch. 3 to the Act. The local authority can take action by agreement with the person served with the notice, or on their own without agreement. If acting with agreement the local authority takes an all the rights of the person on whom the notice was served in connection to the work in terms of being able to access the property and can then charge the cost of any work done back to that person.

If the date for starting works has not been complied with, or the local authority believes that there has been a lack of progress on the works, the local authority may take matters into their own hands. If the local authority intends to take action themselves, then they must serve a notice of their intention to do so before they enter into the premises (para. 4). Such a notice must be served sufficiently in advance that there is reasonable notice of the authority's intention and must be served on the person who was originally served with the Improvement Notice and must also be served on the occupier of the premises. It must set out:

- the Improvement Notice to which it relates;
- the premises which the authority intends to enter;
- the hazard or hazards they wish to remedy;
- that the authority intends to enter the premises;
- what action the authority intends to take on the premises;
- the power that the authority is relying on to enter into the premises and take action (Sch. 3, in other words).

Once seven days has elapsed from such a notice being served, or if local authority workmen are on site, it is an offence, punishable at level 4 on the standard scale, for a person served with the notice to carry out works or to employ someone else to carry out any works at the premises. It is a defence to show that the works were urgently required to prevent danger to occupiers of the premises.

Recovery of charges and expenses on enforcement action

Under s. 49 and Sch. 3 local authorities are entitled to make reasonable charges and recover monies in respect of expenses incurred for:

- serving an Improvement Notice;
- making a Prohibition Order or an Emergency Prohibition Order;
- serving an HAN;
- taking emergency remedial action;
- making a Demolition Order.

The expenses that can be recovered are those incurred in:

- determining whether to serve the Notice or Order or whether to take the action;
- serving the Notice or Order;
- in the case of an HAN or Improvement Notice, identifying the necessary works to be specified in the Notice.

A local authority is also able to recover expenses associated with the carrying out of any annual review required and for the cost of serving copies of the decision of such a review. Although the Act specifies that the charges cannot exceed an amount to be determined by the appropriate national authority, no such maximum amount had been set at the time of writing.

Where local authorities have taken enforcement action on an Improvement Notice without agreement, they are empowered to recover their expenses in so doing. Local authorities can seek to recover their expenses direct from the landlord of a property or by requiring the landlord's agent or the tenant or licensee of the premises to make payments of the rent direct to the local authority. The expenses and interest on them are a charge over the premises, and the local authority has the same powers in respect of that charge as a mortgagee by deed under the *Law of Property Act* 1925.

The first stage in the recovery of expenses is the service of a demand for those expenses by the local authority. Such a demand must be served on the landlord and/or on any person who collects rent on the landlord's behalf. If the local authority does not serve a demand on either of these two persons, then they cannot recover monies from them.

If a demand is served on an agent and they can show that they have only held a limited sum of money (being less than the total of the demand) on behalf of their client since the date of service of the demand, then the agent's liability is limited to the sum that they hold.

Once a demand has been served, the person who has been served has 21 days to appeal, after which the demand becomes operative. Once the demand has become operative the expenses and interest become a local land charge over the property and the local authority will be able to exercise a power of sale under the *Law of Property Act* 1925, or the authority can choose to serve a notice on the tenant or licensee under para. 12.

Once a demand has become operative, the local authority is empowered to serve a recovery notice on anyone occupying the premises or part of them on a tenancy or licence. Such a notice will require that any rent for the premises is paid direct to the local authority until such time as the expenses and interest incurred have been paid.

Interest on the expenses accrues from the date of service of the demand, rather than from the date at which it becomes operative. The interest rate is determined by the local authority and the only check on it is that it must be reasonable.

Finally, there is a cleverly inserted para. 14 in the schedule which closes any potential loophole in the ability of the local authority to recover monies. This allows the local authority to apply to a Residential Property Tribunal where they are unlikely to recover monies and they can demonstrate that a person is profiting by virtue of the works done by that authority allowing more persons to occupy the property. In this case the local authority can ask the Tribunal to make an order for such payments as the tribunal 'considers to be just'.

On Appeal the RPT has the ability to make an order 'confirming, questioning, or varying the demand as it considers appropriate' (Sch. 3, para. 11(5)). On the basis of limited decisions so far, it appears that the RPT is reluctant to dispute reasonable charges levied by an authority, particularly where these costs are largely incurred by employment of an external contractor even if the RPT considers the charges to be on the 'high side' (CHI/00HX/HIN/2007/0001).

Recovery of possession

Section 33 of the Act stipulates that the rights of a tenant supplied by the *Rent Act* 1977 or the *Housing Act* 1988 do not prevent the recovery of possession for the purpose of complying with a Notice or Order. It is not clear how this is supposed to work in practice. This could be read to mean that a Notice or Order requiring works permits a landlord to ignore the security of tenure granted to protected or assured tenants and may evict them simply by service of a notice to quit.

Alternatively, it might mean that the court must have regard to the existence of such a notice when deciding whether to award possession.

It is the authors' view that, unpalatable though it may be, the former view is correct. Courts are likely to be very reluctant to permit a landlord who is likely to have permitted property to fall into disrepair to circumvent their tenants' security of tenure in this way. As a result a landlord is likely to have to produce very cogent evidence that any eviction is 'for the purpose of complying with a Notice or Order'.

Other enforcement action

There are a number of other possible enforcement options available with regard to Improvement Notices and Prohibition Orders.

Where a Prohibition Order has come into effect, a lessor or lessee of a property can apply to the RPTS for the lease to be determined or varied. It is a requirement of such proceedings that the RPTS give any sub-lessee of the property the opportunity to be heard. Such an order may be absolute or be subject to terms and conditions, and may particularly include conditions regarding the payment of compensation or damages, where appropriate.

There are also powers for a magistrates' court to order an occupier or any other relevant person, such as a manager, licence holder, or other person having control of the premises, to allow access or do anything else which will assist the carrying out of works where they are obstructing a local authority from carrying out necessary works under an Improvement Notice or Prohibition Order. Once such an order has been made, the person obstructing the authority will be liable to a fine of £20 for each day or part-day that the obstruction continues.

The magistrates' court also has the power to allow the owner of a property which is prejudiced by the failure of another person to take action to make an application for access to do works specified in the notice. The court must be convinced that the applicant is being prejudiced by a failure to carry out works.

Emergency action

Local authorities can take emergency action if they consider that a category 1 hazard exists on a premises and:

- they are satisfied that the hazard poses an imminent risk to the health and safety of the occupiers of the premises or other residential premises; and
- there is no management order in force in respect of the premises.

Service of Notices and Orders

The service of Improvement Notices is dealt with in Part I of Sch. I to the Act, which also applies to Hazard Awareness Notices. The service of Prohibition Orders is dealt with by Part I of Sch. II. The requirements for service of Prohibition Orders are more stringent and require more people to be served, reflecting their more serious nature.

Improvement and Hazard Awareness Notices should be served on the licence holder if the property is licensed under Parts II or III of the Act. Where the property is not licensed, the Notice should be served on the person having control of the property or on the owner if the property is a flat or, if the property is an HMO, then the notice can be served either on the person who has control of the HMO or on the person who manages the HMO.

The definitions of 'person having control' and 'person managing' a property are set out in s. 263. The person having control of a property is the person who receives the rent for themselves or on behalf of someone else, and therefore usually this will mean a managing agent. The person managing the property is the person who ultimately receives the rent. In cases where there is no managing agent the two people may, of course, be the same. Copies of Improvement and Hazard Awareness Notices are also required to be served on any occupier of a premises as well as on any person who has an interest as a freeholder, lessee, or mortgagee. These copies must be served within seven days of the service of the original notice. Therefore in the case of a flat let through a managing agent, a Notice would need to be served on the landlord, agent, occupier, and freehold head landlord, and on any mortgagee of the landlord. It is not currently clear whether a failure to serve the necessary copies would invalidate the original Notice, but it would be unlikely that a RPT could be persuaded to take such a view.

Appealing Notices and Orders

Notices and Orders must be appealed to the Residential Property Tribunal Service. This process is described in more detail in Chapter 11. There are time limits for appeals, which vary depending on the type of Notice or Order being served. These time limits are discussed further in Appendix H.

Improvement Notices and HANs can only be appealed by those on whom the Notice has been served, and not by an individual who has been served with a copy of a notice. The right to appeal notices conferred by provisions regarding HMOs under the *Housing Act* 1985 was not carried over into the *Housing Act* 2004, and therefore a tenant has no right to appeal an Improvement Notice or, by extension, an HAN (CHI/23 UB/HIN/2007/0002). Prohibition Orders, however, can be appealed by occupiers.

Disrepair and the HHSRS

One of the key points to remember with regard to the HHSRS is that it is not the same as disrepair. Many properties that will be required to have work done under the HHSRS will not be in disrepair as it is legally understood. For a more extensive discussion of disrepair, see Jason Hunter, *Case in Point: Dilapidations* (RICS Books). Therefore the HHSRS can require a landlord to do far more than merely put a house in repair.

So, for example the Court of Appeal has decided that a landlord was not liable under the *Defective Premises Act* 1972 because the glass in a property did not comply with current standards for safety glass (see *Alker v Collingwood Housing Association* [2007] EWCA Civ 343). However, under the collision and entrapment hazard profile, a local authority EHO would be within his rights to demand that such glass was upgraded to modern standards. This would still not provide any redress for the individual tenant against the landlord, as was sought in *Alker*. Landlords must be aware that the HHSRS can require that they do far more than they may have had to in the past but, at the same time, tenants must understand that the service of an HHSRS notice on a landlord does not immediately equate to disrepair for which they have a right to seek compensation.

Conclusion

The HHSRS is an enormously important part of the Act. It gives tremendous latitude to local authority EHOs to require alterations to property. More worryingly, many tenants have taken the view that if the local authority finds something that needs doing under the HHSRS, then there must be something wrong with the property for which they are entitled to be compensated. This means that landlords often find themselves embattled on two fronts, dealing with a local authority which demands expensive changes to their property while also being pursued by tenants seeking compensation. There is no sign that courts have been sympathetic to tenants making such claims. Were they to do so the HHSRS would have reached even further than intended.

Part 2

Houses in Multiple Occupation and Licensing

2

What is an HMO?

Both entire buildings and parts of buildings may be HMOs. In this chapter the word 'building' will be used in the obvious way to include both possibilities. For example, living accommodation above a shop could constitute an HMO.

In order to decide whether a building, or a part of a building, is an HMO, the following process should be followed:

1 Apply each of the five tests set out in the *Housing Act* 2004. If none of the tests applies, the building is not an HMO.
2 Check if it is covered by one of the categories of exceptions set out in the act or in regulations. If it is covered, it is not an HMO.

The five tests for an HMO

- The 'standard test' – this covers most houses where two or more households share basic amenities.
- The 'self-contained flat test' – this is very similar to the standard test but applies to self-contained flats.
- The 'converted buildings test' – a building which has been converted into units of living accommodation that are not themselves self-contained flats.
- Buildings subject to an 'HMO declaration': where homes would otherwise satisfy the standard, self-contained flat or converted buildings test, but where there are other uses of the accommodation other than as living accommodation, the authority can make an HMO declaration that makes the building an HMO anyway.
- Converted blocks of flats.

This chapter will begin by explaining a number of common terms used by more than one of the tests, and then examine each test in detail.

Households, families and relatives

Both the standard and self-contained flat tests use the concept of a 'household', which in turn depends on the legal definitions of 'family' and 'relative' in the *Housing Act* 2004.

Two people will not be considered as being members of the same household unless either they are members of the same family, or one of a number of other conditions is satisfied.

A foster child and foster parent living in the same building or a part of a building are treated as forming a single household, but only if the child was placed with their foster parent under the *Fostering Services Regulations* 2002 (in Wales this is the *Fostering Services (Wales) Regulations* 2002), according to the *Licensing and Management of Houses in Multiple Occupation and Other Houses (Miscellaneous Provisions) (England) Regulations* 2006 (SI 2006/373) and the *Licensing and Management of Houses in Multiple Occupation and Other Houses (Miscellaneous Provisions) (Wales) Regulations* 2006 (SI 2006/1715 (W.177)), reg. 4(2).

This would appear to cause difficulty to families where a foster child who was fostered before the regulations came into force has since remained with their family without being adopted, a circumstance which is not uncommon.

Similarly a person receiving care and that person's carer who are living together in the same building or part of a building are treated as forming a single household under the *Licensing and Management of Houses in Multiple Occupation and Other Houses (Miscellaneous Provisions) (England) Regulations* 2006 (SI 2006/373) and the *Licensing and Management of Houses in Multiple Occupation and Other Houses (Miscellaneous Provisions) (Wales) Regulations* 2006 (SI 2006/1715 (W.177)), reg. 4(1), but only where the care is supplied under an adult placement agreement pursuant to the *Adult Placement Schemes Regulations* 2004 (in Wales the *Adult Schemes (Wales) Regulations* 2004.

Families and relatives

The members of a person's family are:
- their relatives;
- their partner and partner's relatives;
- any of their relatives' partners;
- any of their relatives' partners' relatives.

A **relative** is any of: parent, grandparent, aunt, uncle, sibling, nephew, niece or cousin. Both step- and half-relations count in the same way as their full relations.

A **partner** is anyone:
- to whom the person is married;
- of the opposite sex with whom they live as husband and wife;
- of the same sex with whom they live in a relationship equivalent to husband and wife.

A **step-child** is treated as if they were a child of their step-parent.

Consider the below chart. In this case Fred and Ginger are living as a couple. Under the Housing Act this means that if Fred's mother (Anne) and Ginger's mother (Margaret) are also living in the property, Anne is not only a member of Ginger's family but also a member of Margaret's family. Naturally the reciprocal relationship will also exist and Margaret is a member of both Fred and Anne's family.

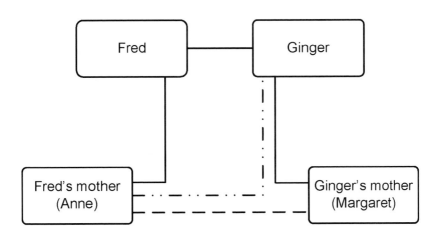

Q. Surely I don't need to know the family relationships of my tenants?

A. If you want to be sure that a property doesn't become an HMO, you do. You may not be guilty of a criminal offence of managing an unlicensed HMO because you would have a reasonable excuse for not licensing the property, but the property would be an HMO even if you were unaware of the family relationships.

It is highly recommended that any tenancy agreement lists permitted occupiers, including children, and states their relationship to any tenant.

Live-in domestic servants

The proper title for this group is 'Persons to be regarded as forming a single household for the purposes of section 254 of the Act: employees'. It applies to a person A (together with any of A's family), living in the same building or part of a building, as some other person B and B's family. They must:

- be performing work of an exclusively domestic nature for either B or a member of B's family who is living with them;
- be supplied with their living accommodation as part of the consideration of carrying out the domestic work;
- not pay any rent or other consideration for their living accommodation.

The Act appears to require that B (the person for whom they are doing the work) is the one supplying them with the living accommodation. One can imagine a number of situations where that would not be the case – for example where a parent is supplied with accommodation and a domestic servant.

There is no explanation of what 'domestic' work might be, but the drafters of the Act clearly had in mind quite a broad interpretation of the word, because they supply a list of people, all of whom are to be considered as doing domestic work under the *Licensing and Management of Houses in Multiple Occupation and Other Houses (Miscellaneous Provisions) (England) Regulations* 2006 (SI 2006/373) and the *Licensing and Management of Houses in Multiple Occupation and Other Houses (Miscellaneous Provisions) (Wales) Regulations* 2006 (SI 2006/1715 (W.177)), reg. 3(3):

- au pair;
- nurse;
- nanny;

- carer;
- governess;
- servant, including maid, butler, cook or cleaner;
- chauffeur;
- gardener;
- secretary
- personal assistant.

In order to decide whether a building is an HMO, first check whether it falls into one of the exceptions listed in Sch. 14 to the Housing Act, and then whether it meets one of the five tests for being an HMO.

Self-contained flats

The first stage of applying the five tests in the *Housing Act 2004* is to identify any self-contained flats in the building in question. Each self-contained flat is considered separately from the rest of the building, and the self-contained flat test is applied to it. The building, disregarding any self-contained flats, is then subjected to the remaining tests.

What is a 'self-contained flat'?

A self-contained flat is a separate set of premises, which does not have to be all on one floor (so 'maisonettes' and other split-level dwellings would be included) and which:
- forms part of (but not the whole of) a building;
- has all three basic amenities available for the exclusive use of the occupants;
- either the whole or a material part of which lies above or below some other part of the building.

The self-contained flat test is satisfied if:

- there are units of living accommodation in the flat;
- those units are occupied by individuals who do not form a single household;
- the living accommodation is occupied as their only or main residence;
- their occupation of the living accommodation constitutes the only use of that accommodation (the 'sole use' condition);
- some consideration (such as rent) is being paid in respect of at least one of the people for their occupation of the accommodation;
- two or more households share at least one basic amenity.

47

Q: One of my properties has a single-storey rear extension that is reachable only through the common parts of the building. Is it a self-contained flat?

A: No. At least a part of a self-contained flat must be above or below another part of the building.

The standard test

The standard test is identical to the self-contained flat test, except that it is applied to the remainder of the building disregarding any self-contained flats in it. The standard test requires that:

- there are units of living accommodation in the building;
- the living accommodation in the building is occupied by individuals who do not form a single household;
- the living accommodation is occupied as their only or main residence;
- their occupation of the living accommodation constitutes the only use of that accommodation (the 'sole use' condition);
- some consideration (such as rent) is being paid in respect of at least one of the people for their occupation of the accommodation;
- two or more households share at least one basic amenity.

Basic amenities
- Toilet
- Personal washing facilities
- Cooking facilities

Converted buildings

Where one or more units of accommodation have been created in the building (or part of building) since it was constructed, it is known as a 'converted building'. In considering whether a converted building is an HMO, any self-contained flats in the building must first be excluded from consideration (as they are for the standard test). If parts of the building have been converted into self-contained flats, not only may each flat be subject to the 'self-contained flat' test, but any other part of the building would also need to be checked against the 'converted block of flats' test, given below.

The 'converted building test' is very similar, but not identical to, the standard test, with the significant difference that there is no requirement that households are sharing at least one basic amenity.

A converted building meets the 'converted building test' if:

- there are units of living accommodation in the building which do not consist of self-contained flats;
- that living accommodation in the building is occupied by individuals who do not form a single household;
- those individuals occupy the living accommodation as their only or main residence;
- their occupation of the living accommodation constitutes the only use of that accommodation (the 'sole use' condition);
- some consideration (such as rent) is being paid in respect of at least one of the people for their occupation of the accommodation.

Only or main residence

Certain groups of people are 'treated as' occupying accommodation as their only or main residence. They are:

- students – those who occupy the building for the purposes of full-time study in higher education;
- those occupying the accommodation as a refuge.

What is a refuge?

A refuge is a building (or a part of a building), which is:
- managed by a voluntary organisation; and
- used wholly or mainly for the temporary accommodation of people who have left their homes as a result of physical violence or mental abuse (or the threat of such violence or abuse) where the violence or abuse came from, or was threatened by, their spouse or someone with whom they were cohabiting.

'Cohabiting' appears to be restricted to those in a relationship akin to marriage and so would exclude others abused by those they live with.

Occupation is the sole use of the accommodation

Where the sole use condition is not met, a local authority still has a power to bring the building or flat into the definition of an

HMO. If a local authority is satisfied that one of the 'standard', 'self-contained flat' or 'converted building' tests would apply if the sole use condition were satisfied, then if the authority also consider that the occupation by persons who do not form a single household constitutes a significant use of the accommodation (the 'significant usage' condition), it may make an 'HMO declaration'.

There is a presumption that the sole use condition and significant use conditions are met.

Converted blocks of flats

The last test is the 'converted blocks of flats' test. As will be explained in Chapters 3 and 4, the rules for licensing and management of HMOs which meet the converted blocks of flats test are different from those that meet the first four tests.

If the whole or part of the building has been converted into self-contained flats, then the whole block will be an HMO (whether or not the individual flats are HMOs) if:

- fewer than two-thirds of the self-contained flats are owner-occupied; and
- the building work undertaken in connection with the conversion did not comply with the 'appropriate' building standard.

Here 'owner-occupier' means anyone with a long lease of 21 or more years, a freeholder, or a member of a leaseholder or freeholder's family.

Appropriate building standards

The appropriate building standards depend on when the building work was done.

If it was completed before 1 June 1992 or was dealt with by reg. 20 of the *Building Regulations* 1991 (SI 1991/2768), and would not have been exempt under those regulations, the appropriate building standards are equivalent to those imposed, in relation to a building or part of a building to which those regulations applied, by those regulations as they had effect on 1 June 1992.

In the case of any other converted block of flats, the appropriate building standards are those imposed on it under s. 1 of the *Building Act* 1984.

Exceptions from the definition of HMO

The definition of an HMO given so far is used as it is in Part I of the *Housing Act* 2004 – in other words, when dealing with the housing, health and safety rating system. For all other purposes, there are a number of exceptions, given in Sch. 14 of the *Housing Act* 2004, so that even if a building satisfies one of the five tests given in the act, it may not be an HMO. The most significant exceptions are as follows.

Buildings controlled or managed by public sector bodies.

Here 'public sector body' includes local housing authorities, registered social landlords, police authorities (including the Metropolitan Police Authority), fire and rescue authorities and health service bodies.

Buildings regulated otherwise than under the Housing Act 2004

This exception covers buildings such as prisons, care and children's homes which are already regulated by a tight statutory scheme. A full list may be found in Sch. 1 to the *Licensing and Management of Houses in Multiple Occupation and Other Houses (Miscellaneous Provisions) (England) Regulations* 2006 and the equivalent Welsh regulations.

Student accommodation

This exception is for student accommodation controlled by the academic institution at which the student is studying. The requirement is that the accommodation is occupied solely or principally by persons who occupy it for the purpose of undertaking a full-time course of further or higher education.

Presumably 'married' accommodation (where one partner is not a student) supplied by a university or college would be 'principally' occupied, even if the student was in a minority, which might occur where there were children of the family as well.

Religious communities

Similarly there is an exception for a building occupied principally for the purposes of a religious community whose principal occupation is prayer, contemplation, education or the relief of suffering.

Owner occupiers

This is likely to be an important exception. It occurs when the building is occupied by people who own either a leasehold (granted for a term of more than 21 years) or freehold interest in the property, together with members of their households and no more than two other people.

Q: I am advising friends who have bought a house to share. They are unrelated; does that mean that the property is an HMO?

A: Normally, no. Provided the only people living in the house are the friends, members of their families and up to two other unrelated people, the property will not be an HMO.

Buildings occupied by two people

If a building is occupied by only two people, then it is not an HMO.

3

Licensing of HMOs and other properties

Two types of HMO

HMO classifications fall into two categories: those defined by s. 254 and those defined by s. 257 of the *Housing Act*. They are usually known as s. 254 and s. 257 HMOs. Without going into details, s. 254 HMOs meet one of the first four tests given in the previous chapter. They are normally rented properties occupied by three or more individuals who form more than one family. Section 257 HMOs are buildings the conversion of which into multiple dwellings was not in accordance with the *Building Regulations* 1991, and which are still not in accordance with these regulations, and where more than one-third of the property is rented out. Note that a building can be an HMO under s. 257 while individual flats within that building may or may not be HMOs under s. 254.

Q: Do all HMOs need a licence?
A: No. It is important to realise that a property can be an HMO without ever needing to be licensed. Only certain types of high-risk HMO are required to have a licence, and there will be a great many properties that will be HMOs but which will not require licensing. **It is important to note, however, that unlicensed HMOs will need to comply with the management regulations for HMOs**; see below.

Q: Do residential properties other than HMOs need a licence?
A: Sometimes. In some areas the local housing authority may have designated other classes of residential accommodation that need licensing. This is known as 'selective residential licensing'. The rules on licensing and management are the same as for s. 254 HMOs.

Licensing

There are three categories of HMO licensing which apply to s. 254 HMOs. These are:

- mandatory;
- additional;
- transitional.

In the case of additional and transitional licensing, the local authority has a great deal of discretion as to which HMOs it will apply the licensing scheme. The local authority has no discretion as to the applicability of mandatory licensing, the breadth of which is covered by regulation.

What constitutes an occupier?

An occupier is any individual who counts a property as their residence. Note that it does not have to be their main residence and they do not have to be the tenant of the property. The age of the individual is equally unimportant. So babies and children are occupiers, for the purposes of HMO considerations.

Mandatory licensing is required for certain classes of HMO, set out by SI 2006/371 in England and SI 2006/1712 in Wales. The requirements are the same, and state that HMOs which:

- have five or more occupiers; and
- comprise of three or more storeys

must have a licence.

Additional licensing allows local authorities to designate other classes of HMO in some or all of their areas of responsibility as subject to licensing. This power is governed by ss. 56 to 60 of the Housing Act. Any local authority that wishes to make such a designation must gain central government approval.

Local authorities must believe that a significant proportion of HMOs in the area concerned are being managed ineffectively such that it is causing one or more problems for HMO occupiers or the public. They must take reasonable steps to consult those who might be affected by such a designation and consider any representations made. The local authority must ensure that such a designation is consistent with its overall housing strategy and must also consider whether they can achieve the same effect by another means and whether a designation will actually assist them in dealing with problems they have identified.

At the time of writing, no local authority has sought to make such a designation, but there is clear scope for a judicial review application if a local authority were to make such a designation without carrying out appropriate consultations, or failed to make proper notification of such a designation being made.

Transitional licensing is a product of SI 2006/1060 (SI 2006/1535 for Wales). This allows for local authorities which previously operated an approved licensing scheme under the auspices of the *Housing Act* 1985 (the 'old Act') to continue to operate such a scheme under the *Housing Act* 2004 (the 'new Act'). These schemes will continue to have the same ambit as before and will simply take on the prosecution and standards requirements from the new Act. Landlords who were previously members of schemes under the old Act that have been transitioned will have their licences 'passported' into the scheme operating under the new Act. A large number of London boroughs have made use of the transitional provisions, but they are not widely used outside London.

Calculating storeys

It is important to be able to work out how many storeys a property has. This is vital for working out whether or not the HMO falls into a licensing scheme. The basis on which the number of storeys is calculated is set out in SI 2006/371 in England (SI 2006/1712 in Wales). Again, they are the same.

The number of storeys is the number contained in the individual HMO, rather than the building. Therefore a single-storey flat within a four-storey block of flats is a one-storey property and not a four-storey property, as long as it is distinct and self-contained.

Any storey which is used or has been adapted for use wholly or partly as living accommodation or which is being used in connection with and is 'an integral part of the HMO' must be counted when calculating the number of storeys. This includes mezzanine floors that are more than simply a turning point in a flight of stairs. Therefore a two-floor house with a loft conversion will count as a three-storey property. Likewise, a two-storey house where an individual is using the loft to sleep in will also count as a three-storey property.

Basements and attics which have been constructed, converted or adapted for use wholly or partly as living accommodation must be counted even if they are, for the time being, empty.

Basements which form the principal entry to the HMO must also be counted, even if there is no living accommodation on that level. Therefore a mews house with a ground floor entrance and parking, with two storeys of living accommodation above, will be counted as a three-storey property.

Business premises above or below a property must always be counted as part of the HMO, even if they are not connected. So a two-storey maisonette above a ground-floor shop will be counted as a three-storey property, regardless of the fact that the two may be entirely unconnected and even have different owners. Their physical juxtaposition, one above another, is sufficient to bring them together for the purposes of the HMO regulations.

There are some difficulties when calculating the number of storeys in a property, and different local authorities take different viewpoints. So, in some areas a local authority will consider an unconverted loft space to be an 'integral part of the HMO', as it can be used for storage purposes unless there is a notice affixed to it stating that it is not to be used. Other local authorities will take a more relaxed view. A similar issue occurs with regard to split-level floors. Some local authorities will always consider these as two separate storeys, while others will consider the degree of vertical separation. These differences of interpretation offer fertile ground for an appeal to the RPT.

Further difficulties have arisen as a result of a prosecution in relation to a property in Cirencester (*Cotswold District Council v Roderick Williams*, Gloucester Magistrates' Court, 4 January 2008). This concerned a property which comprised the first and second floors of a house. The ground floor comprised of a quite separate self-contained flat which was owned by somebody else. The top two floors were an HMO, but it was argued by the landlord that the property was not a three-storey property and not therefore subject to mandatory licensing. The council argued that SI 2006/371 sets out which properties are subject to mandatory licensing and how to calculate storeys for that purpose. Paragraph 3(3)(f) requires that 'any other storey that is used wholly or partly as living accommodation or partly as living accommodation or in connection with, and as an integral part of, the HMO' should be counted. The council stated that the phrase 'any other storey used wholly or partly as living accommodation' should be read in isolation, and that this was sufficient to ensure that the separate ground-floor flat should be counted. This argument was successful in court and the landlord was successfully prosecuted. The authors feel that this argument is erroneous. As the council itself accepted, it is perverse to suggest that an HMO can comprise of more storeys than it actually contains. It is also the case that s. 254 states that 'a building or part of a building' is an HMO if it meets a series of tests. The fact that a part of a building can be an HMO by itself indicates an intention that buildings should not necessarily be considered as a whole unless their structure warrants it. SI 2006/371 does set out a situation where parts of a building outside the HMO should be counted in paragraphs 3(3)(c) and (d), in relation to business premises and it does so in very specific language which is not replicated in paragraph 3(3)(f). If it was the intent that other storeys should be counted then similar specificity would be expected. As this book goes to press, this matter is the subject of an appeal the outcome of which is unknown. If it is the case that separate self-contained premises should be counted when considering the number of storeys in a property, then a large number of properties that were not believed to require licensing will find themselves falling into the licensing requirements.

Selective licensing of other residential accommodation

Selective licensing allows local authorities to introduce licensing schemes for rental property other than HMOs. As with additional licensing, central government must approve any such scheme. Such a designation cannot be made unless one of the following conditions are satisfied. These are that:

- the area is, or is likely to become, an area of low housing demand and the making of a designation, in conjunction with other measures, will contribute to the improvement of social or economic conditions in the area; or
- the area experiences anti-social behaviour which private-sector landlords have not taken reasonable steps to combat, and the making of a designation, in conjunction with other measures, would reduce or eliminate the problem.

The Act allows further conditions to be made by Statutory Instrument. No further conditions exist in England, but in Wales SI 2006/2825 sets out further conditions which will allow a local authority to apply for selective licensing. These are that:

- a local housing authority has declared an area as a renewal area under s. 89 of the *Local Government and Housing Act* 1989; or
- a local housing authority has provided assistance to any person in accordance with an adopted and published policy under the *Regulatory Reform (Housing Assistance) (England and Wales) Order* 2002 in that area (power of local housing authorities to provide assistance); or
- the area of their district or area in their district comprises a minimum of 25% of housing stock let by private sector landlords.

In June 2007 Salford City Council became the first local authority to introduce a selective licensing scheme. This scheme requires that all private landlords in certain areas of Salford must have a licence, irrespective of whether or not their property is an HMO.

The process for applying for a licence for a property under a selective licensing scheme is identical to that used for an HMO.

Section 257 licensing

Originally, s. 257 HMOs continued to be licensed under the old regime from the *Housing Act* 1985. However, the introduction of SI 2007/1904 in England and SI 2007/3231 in Wales has allowed for local authorities to introduce licensing schemes for s. 257 HMOs in the same way that they would go about introducing an additional licensing scheme as discussed above. As with additional licensing, central government permission is required before any such scheme can be introduced. There are transitional provisions in operation which will allow local authorities which operate s. 257 licensing schemes under the old *Housing Act* 1985 system to continue to do so until October 2008. After that date, any local authority wishing to license s. 257 HMOs will have to do so under the *Housing Act* 2004.

The systems of licensing for s. 257 HMOs are basically the same as for the licensing of s. 254 HMOs. This has come about due to partial amendments to the Housing Act made by SI 2007/1903 and SI 2007/3231. These Statutory Instruments slightly amend the Housing Act for the purpose of determining licensing applications for s. 257 HMOs **only**. The key portion of the Housing Act in both its original form as it applies to s. 254 HMOs and in its amended form as it applies to s. 257 HMOs can be found in Appendix C. The procedural rules and management regulations for s. 254 HMOs and properties covered by selective licensing are identical; those for s. 257 HMOs are different.

Gaining a licence

The process of applying for and being granted a licence is dealt with in ss. 63–68 of the Housing Act. The detail of the application process and the standards that local authorities are required to consider when deciding whether to grant or refuse a licence are set out in SI 2006/373 for England and SI 2006/1715 (W.177) for Wales. There are some differences between the regulations for England and Wales, primarily relating to the differing standards that a licensable property is required to meet, but these are relatively minor.

Each local authority has its own forms and procedure for making an application, although there are substantial similarities between all of them. All the licence applications are long and require a great deal of detail as to the property and those who will be involved in managing it. Frustratingly, some local authorities do not appear to be acting entirely within the regulations and are asking for certain information or certifications to which they are not entitled under the regulations.

The application process

The process of applying for a licence is relatively straightforward, if a little bureaucratic. Most local authorities have made their HMO licence application forms available through their websites, and this will probably be the easiest way for a landlord to obtain the necessary paperwork.

Once the form has been completed, it is simply a matter of returning it to the authority along with the appropriate fee. Note that local authorities are usually very strict regarding licence applications and will tend to return any application that is not completed in full. Under reg. 7(7) of SI 2006/373 (SI

2006/1715 in Wales), the fee is fully refundable should the property turn out not to have required a licence at the time the application was made. The moral is that applications should always be made whenever there is any doubt as to whether a property requires a licence, on the basis that the fee can always be recovered if it turns out later that it was not required.

Once an application has been made, a landlord has a defence against a charge of operating an unlicensed HMO (under ss. 72–75) or an unlicensed property that is subject to selective residential licensing (under ss. 95–98) so long as:

- the local authority has not yet decided whether to grant a licence or temporary exemption notice; or
- if the local authority has rejected the application then the period for making an appeal has not yet expired or an appeal has been lodged which has yet to be determined.

This leads to the surprising situation where a landlord could apply for a licence, issue a s. 21 notice on the strength of that application and then, assuming the local authority was not very prompt in its decision-making, recover possession of the property, thereby obviating the need for the licence in the first place! However, it is unlikely that the licence fee would be recoverable as at the time the application was made the property would have been liable for a licence.

It is the usual practice of most local authorities to issue a confirmation that an application has been made, although there is no requirement for them to do so.

Information required

The information needed on an application form is prescribed in Sch. 2 of SI 2006/373 and SI 2006/1715 (W.177) for England and Wales respectively. This Schedule has been modified by the introduction of SI 2007/1903 and SI 2007/3229 to allow for licence application for s. 257 HMOs and the modified version of SI 2006/373 can be found in Appendix A with the changes shown in italics. The amended Welsh version is not provided as it is exactly the same.

Fit and proper person

It is key to a local authority's decision to award a licence that the applicant be a 'fit and proper person'. Section 66 (or s. 89 for selective licensing) of the Housing Act sets out the criteria to be considered as follows:

'(1) In deciding for the purposes of section 64(3)(b) or (d) whether a person (P) is a fit and proper person to be the licence holder or (as the case may be) the manager of the house, the local housing authority must have regard (among other things) to any evidence within subsection (2) or (3).

(2) Evidence is within this subsection if it shows that P has-

(a)   committed any offence involving fraud or other dishonesty, or violence or drugs, or any offence listed in Schedule 3 to the Sexual Offences Act 2003 (c. 42) (offences attracting notification requirements);

(b)   practised unlawful discrimination on grounds of sex, colour, race, ethnic or national origins or disability in, or in connection with, the carrying on of any business;

(c)   contravened any provision of the law relating to housing or of landlord and tenant law; or

(d)   acted otherwise than in accordance with any applicable code of practice approved under section 233.

(3) Evidence is within this subsection if-

(a)   it shows that any person associated or formerly associated with P (whether on a personal, work or other basis) has done any of the things set out in subsection (2)(a) to (d), and

(b)   it appears to the authority that the evidence is relevant to the question whether P is a fit and proper person to be the licence holder or (as the case may be) the manager of the house.'

Criminal records

Some local authorities have sought to carry out criminal record checks on all applicants by requiring applicants to provide a certificate obtained through Disclosure Scotland (checks through the Criminal Records Bureau cannot be carried out in this manner). The CLG have provided guidance on this issue to LACORS (the Local Authorities Coordinators of Regulatory Services) which has clarified that this practice should not be routine. They state that:

'there was never a policy intention that local authorities should routinely require criminal record checks to be carried out. That is simply not necessary, since there is a presumption that the applicant is fit and proper unless there is evidence to the contrary.'

Clearly local authorities that carry out such checks as a matter of routine are acting contrary to the policy intent of the CLG. According to LACORS, a failure 'to provide a Disclosure Scotland form could lead to refusal of a licence application followed by prosecution for not licensing the HMO. However, in refusing an application on the grounds the landlord was not a fit and proper person, the council must be satisfied that evidence exists to justify this approach. The landlord could appeal against the council's decision to refuse the licence application' (see www.lacors.gov.uk/lacors/ContentDetails.aspx? id=16819).

It is a criminal offence for a person to make a dishonest application by failing to disclose details of any criminal convictions and Local Authorities should rely on these penalties in the first instance to ensure compliance with the law. However, it still seems that many local authorities consider a Disclosure Scotland certificate to be an essential requirement, and anecdotal evidence suggests that most local authorities will reject out of hand applications in which the prospective licence holder discloses any form of criminal conviction, irrespective of its relevance to the licence application.

Currently no appeals to the RPT have been taken on this issue so it is not yet clear what will happen. It should also be noted that the requirement to disclose convictions is not intended to apply to those convictions that are 'spent' under the *Rehabilitation of Offenders Act* 1974.

Criteria for deciding applications

Once the local authority is in receipt of a valid application and has decided that the licence holder is suitable, it must consider whether the property is suitable and whether it should grant or refuse the issue of a licence or whether certain conditions should be attached to that licence. The decision-making criteria and the standards to which those criteria must be met are set out in regulations, but these differ slightly between England and Wales. It is not up to local authorities to consider issues that fall outside of the broad statutory criteria.

For example, the fact that a landlord's mortgage forbids the property being used as an HMO is irrelevant to the grant or refusal of a licence (LON/00AH/HML/2007/0001).

Regulations have set out the minimum standards which local authorities must enforce, but they are free to set their own further standards as they deem appropriate. However, in CHI/00MR/HML/2007/0001 the RPT cautioned against rigid adherence to standards, pointing out that standards beyond the minimum can 'only be taken as some guidance or aspiration as to what might be suitable' and that it was necessary to consider 'each case on its own facts'. They also highlighted that the Housing Act only requires that accommodation be 'reasonably' suitable and that it does not, therefore, have to be a perfect example of the type to qualify.

England: standards

Under s. 65 of the Housing Act, local authorities are to have regard to certain standards in deciding whether to grant a licence. These standards are set out in more detail within Sch. 3 to SI 2006/373. This schedule has been the object of a great deal of argument and has been modified by SI 2007/1903. The schedule, with the amendments included, is set out in full in Appendix B.

What is a unit?

There has been some uncertainty about what is meant by a unit of accommodation in the regulations. There are many different types of HMO that can exist, from purpose-built bedsits to ordinary houses that happen to be occupied by several unrelated individuals. LACORS has suggested that a unit could be any of: a bed-sit, a bedroom in a shared house, or a self-contained flat.

In LON/00AG/HML/2007/0002 (a case involving the requirement for washing facilities in each unit of accommodation), the RPT did not agree. It refused to accept that a bedroom in a shared house could be described as a unit of living accommodation and drew a distinction between accommodation which is intended to be used for living and that intended only for sleeping. The RPT felt that the government would have to be 'clear and unambiguous' if it wished to 'impose potentially onerous conditions' on house owners.

In CAM/38UB/HML/2007/0001 the RPT declined to follow this reasoning. In the first place, one tribunal decision is not binding on another (while they may be persuasive) and also the detailed facts were different.

It is the authors' view that LACORS is correct in its analysis and is likely to be followed in future RPT cases. The legislation clearly does impose quite stringent conditions on the landlords of HMOs and there is no reason to suppose that tenants living in a shared house, rather than a bedsit, were intended to have reduced protection. The government's decision to remove the requirement for wash-basins in each bedroom will make this a less contentious and onerous condition for landlords in any case.

Schedule 3 of the regulations sets out the factors that the local authority must consider when deciding to grant a licence. The schedule is a curious mix, in that it is in part highly prescriptive but leaves wide areas open to the discretion of the local authority. The schedule sets out that local authorities must ensure that kitchens have fire blankets, fridges with freezer space, extractor fans and the like, but only specifies that the kitchen must be of adequate size and layout, leaving it to individual local authorities to decide how to interpret this.

England, summary of standards

Adequate space heating

Adequate bathrooms, toilets and hand-basins

Hand-basin with splashback in each unit where practicable

Hot and cold water in all baths and toilets and basins

Adequate kitchen with (for shared kitchens) suitable and sufficient:
- Sinks with draining boards
- Hot and cold water
- Worktops
- Refrigerators with suitable freezer space
- Cupboards
- Electrical sockets
- Cooking appliances
- Refuse disposal
- Extractor fans

Appropriate fire precaution facilities

Wales: standards

The standards for Wales are set out in SI 2006/1715 and are almost exactly the same as those for England. However, HMOs in Wales have the advantage that they have never required a sink to be placed in each bedroom where there are five or more occupiers. Here the Welsh regulations display the advantage of being made after the English ones and have benefited from observation of the reaction to the regulations as introduced in

England. They were further modified by SI 2007/3229 to bring them into closer accord with the English system. Therefore Sch. 3 of the Welsh regulations is precisely the same as that for the English regulations, with the exception of paragraph 2:

'2.—(1) Where all or some of the units of living accommodation in an HMO do not contain bathing and toilet facilities for the exclusive use of each individual household, there must be an adequate number of bathrooms, toilets and wash-hand basins suitable for personal washing for the number of persons sharing those facilities, having regard to the age and character of the HMO, the size and layout of each flat and its existing provision for wash-hand basins, toilets and bathrooms.

(3) All bathrooms in an HMO must be suitably and adequately heated and ventilated.

(4) All bathrooms and toilets in an HMO must be of an adequate size and layout.

(5) All baths, toilets and wash hand basins in an HMO must be fit for the purpose.

(6) All bathrooms and toilets in an HMO must be suitably located in or in relation to the living accommodation in the HMO.'

Wales, summary of standards

Adequate space heating

Adequate bathrooms, toilets and hand-basins

Suitable location of bathrooms and toilets and adequate heating of bathrooms

Hot and cold water in all baths and toilets and basins

Adequate kitchen with (for shared kitchens) suitable and sufficient:
- Sinks with draining boards
- Hot and cold water
- Worktops
- Refrigerators with suitable freezer space
- Cupboards
- Electrical sockets
- Cooking appliances
- Refuse disposal
- Extractor fans

Appropriate fire precaution facilities

Schedule 3 standards

The standards laid out by Sch. 3 have caused a great deal of concern for HMO landlords and have led to a number of appeals to the RPT, and so it is worth examining them in detail. The two most important relate to the need for sinks and the requirement for a property to be fire safe, so these will be explored in the most detail.

Sinks

The changes introduced by SI 2007/1903 and SI 2007/3229 represent a significant weakening of the original requirement in England to install a sink in every bedroom in HMOs with five or more occupiers. They give far greater scope for individual local authorities to set standards that they feel are appropriate in each area. LACORS has 'strongly welcomed' the changes and has encouraged 'local authorities to reflect on these changes and decide whether they want to amend their adopted amenity standards' (see www.lacors.gov.uk/lacors/ContentDetails.aspx?id=16980). The changes have substantially reduced the expense of operating a medium-sized HMO for private landlords. In cases where local authorities are seeking the installation of sinks in bedrooms, the requirement should be carefully evaluated in the light of this reduced standard and the comments made by the RPT. In particular, consideration should be given to the amount of washing space already provided, the space reductions in individual rooms that will follow from the installation of further sinks, and the complexity of the works necessary to fulfil these requirements. All of these points were brought up in CHI/00HN/HML/2007/0002 and the RPT was persuaded by these arguments. Naturally, the reduced requirement to provide 'adequate' facilities will have to be codified by local authorities and will again prove a significant area of appeal.

Fire safety

The schedule imposes the rather nebulous requirement that the HMO must have 'appropriate fire precaution facilities and equipment'. Unfortunately this has not been further specified and therefore local authorities have set their own standards. It was originally thought that the *Regulatory Reform (Fire Safety) Order* 2005 (SI 2005/1541) would apply to all HMOs, but it contains an exemption for single private dwellings. Further guidance is awaited from the CLG but it is thought that single properties that happen to be HMOs by virtue of their current usage will be exempt from this Order.

The Chief Fire Officers Association is understood to be working on a guide to necessary fire standards in properties not affected by the RRFSO. However, it is currently up to individual authorities to set their own standards for fire safety in HMOs and most have chosen to adopt a standard similar to that laid down by the guidance to the RRFSO. This requires as a minimum:

- kitchens to have fire extinguishers and fire blankets;
- interlinked mains-powered smoke detectors to be fitted in the common parts of the HMO;
- sleeping areas to have doors with a 30-minute fire rating and which should be fitted with automatic closing devices;
- escape routes to be usable for a minimum of 30 minutes.

The Chartered Institute for Environmental Health has produced a protocol for use by local authorities and fire and rescue authorities to help improve fire safety (see www.cieh.org/library/Knowledge/Housing/Fire%20Protocol%20 final.pdf) and LACORS has encouraged all local authorities to adopt this. Depending on the size of the HMO and the local authority concerned, other requirements may be added. Kitchens which are open-plan or must be passed to exit the property seem to be a particular bug-bear for many local authority inspectors, and they will usually seek to have these enclosed or even moved.

Room size

Most local authorities have set standards relating to the appropriate sizes for rooms etc. However, the RPT has stated that when considering size issues the suitability of the entire property should be examined and a narrow concentration on whether each room is large enough to meet the local authority standard is unacceptable. In CHI/00MR/HML/2007/0001 the RPT took the view that volume and natural lighting were equally as important as floor area, and rejected the local authority argument that communal space should be provided for occupiers for their health and well-being.

Cooking facilites

The provision of adequate cooking facilities has been key in several cases. It is notable that the requirement to provide somewhere specific for residents to cook does not necessarily extend to providing somewhere specific for them to eat, and kitchen/diners or eating in bedrooms appears to be treated as perfectly acceptable (see CAM/42UD/HML/2006/0001). However, it is clear that adequate cooking facilities should include a hob of some sort and an oven facility as a minimum.

Licensing appeals

Appeals against the granting of or the refusal to grant a licence, or against a refusal to vary or revoke a licence, can be made by an applicant, licence holder, or any other relevant person. Such appeals are made to the Residential Property Tribunal and must be made within 28 days of the date specified on the notice advising of the date the decision was made.

Variation and revocation of licences

Local authorities can vary or revoke licences, should they consider this to be appropriate or on the basis of an application. The process for doing this is set out in Sch. 5 to the Housing Act.

Variation

In order to vary a licence the local authority must serve notice on the licence holder and any other relevant persons stating what the variation is, the reasons for it, and the consultation period. The local authority is required to take into account any responses to their consultation, when making a decision. The local authority does not have to fulfil this notice requirement if the variation they are making is minor. If the local authority has received an application for variation which they intend to refuse, they must follow a similar process. If the local authority has decided to grant the variation then they must, within seven days of the decision being made, serve notice on the licence holder and all relevant persons, setting out the reasons for the decision, the right of appeal, and the appeal period from their decision.

Revocation

While the local authority can choose to revoke a licence of its own volition, it also appears to be possible for anyone to request such a revocation.

If a local authority wishes to revoke a licence they must serve notice on the licence holder and any other relevant persons, stating the reasons why they are intending to revoke the licence, and the consultation period. The local authority is required to take any responses to their consultation into account when making a decision. Such notification requirements can be ignored if the revocation is agreed by the licence holder and the local authority does not believe that the notice is necessary.

If, after taking any responses into account, the local authority decides to revoke a licence they must, within seven days of the decision being made, serve notice on the licence holder and all relevant persons setting out the reasons for the decision, the right of appeal, and the appeal period from their decision.

Any consultation period regarding variation or revocation of licences must not be less than 14 days.

Licence conditions, fees, and other points

Licences can last for a maximum of five years. Most local authorities have used this time period, but one or two are issuing three-year licences. The fee for the licence is set at the local authority's discretion and there is no cap on it, although it should reflect the cost to the authority of running the scheme. This has led to a very wide disparity in fees around the country. If it later transpires that a licence application has been made for a property that did not require a licence, then the local authority is required to refund the licence fee in full.

Local authorities are entitled to place conditions on the licence. Any licence will set out the maximum number of permitted occupiers in the property, while under Sch. 4 to the Housing Act, there are certain conditions that must be on a licence. These require the holder to:

- produce the annual gas safety inspection certificate for authority inspection;

69

- keep the electrical appliances in a safe condition and supply the authority with a declaration of their safety on demand;
- keep the furniture in a safe condition and supply the authority with a declaration of its safety on demand;
- keep the smoke alarms in a proper working order and supply the authority with a declaration of their safety on demand; and
- provide the occupiers with a written statement of the terms on which they occupy the property.

Local authorities are also able to impose other conditions on licences in relation to the management use and occupation of the HMO and its condition and contents.

It is important to understand that a licence is for one HMO and attaches to both the property and the licence holder. If a landlord sells his property, the new landlord will not be able to transfer the licence and will need to make an entirely new HMO application.

Planning issues

There have been a number of difficulties associated with the fact that some HMOs fall into a separate planning category from a normal dwelling. The differing standards used by planning officers and environmental health officers have meant that some local authorities have refused licences on the grounds that the landlord did not hold the right planning consent, while other landlords have gained a licence only to be approached by the planning department and informed that they have violated the planning restrictions attached to their property. The reason for the confusion is apparent if we consider the Schedule to the *Town and Country Planning (Use Classes) Order* 1987 (SI 1987/764). This defines Class C3, Dwellinghouses as follows:

> 'Use as a dwellinghouse (whether or not as a sole or main residence) —
> (a)   by a single person or by people living together as a family, or
> (b)   by not more than 6 residents living together as a single household (including a household where care is provided for residents).'

This is of course different from the definition of an HMO for the purposes of the *Housing Act* 2004 and, more importantly, different from the definition of a property which will require mandatory licensing under the Housing Act. As an aside, it is also notable that the definition of 'household' for the purposes of the two pieces of legislation is entirely different. It is clear from this that there are many HMOs, and many that require licences, that fall into the normal category of dwellinghouses and should not, therefore attract any special planning status.

LACORS has issued guidance on the issue which has helped to clarify some of the problems and the appropriate methods of dealing with them. It is clear from the legislation itself precisely what are the appropriate decision making criteria for awarding an HMO licence and as planning considerations do not fall into these criteria local authorities should not be taking them into consideration when deciding whether or not it is appropriate to grant a licence (see www.lacors.gov.uk/lacors/ContentDetails.aspx?id=16601).

TENs

Under s. 62 of the Housing Act it is open to a local authority to grant a landlord a Temporary Exemption Notice (TEN), providing exemption from the requirement to license a property. Such a notice is only available if the person applying has notified the authority that he intends to take steps to procure that the property is no longer required to be licensed.

CLG has published guidance (see www.communities.gov.uk/publications/housing/licensinghouses) stating that, in their view, it is not acceptable to utilise the TEN provisions in order to avoid or evade licensing. 'Simply a proposal to, or the act of, putting an HMO on the market for sale or reducing the number of occupants will not normally be sufficient for a council to agree to issue a temporary exemption notice.'

This view appears to conflict with a strict interpretation of the Housing Act and it is questionable whether a local authority really has a power to refuse a notice when a landlord is taking steps to ensure that a property is no longer liable to be licensed. In LON/00AH/HMV/2007/0002 the RPT stated that the licensing provisions 'could be onerous for a small landlord' and that the process was designed to allow a small landlord to 'put their affairs in order, including to get out altogether if that is what they want to do.'

If a local authority declines to issue a TEN then they must provide a written response setting out their reasons for refusing to do so and the rights to appeal that decision. Failure to issue such a notice does not prevent an appeal being lodged and the RPT appears to view such a failure unfavourably when considering whether to award the costs of an appeal against the local authority.

An application for a TEN does not later prevent a landlord arguing that the same property is not an HMO and the RPT is not prepared to accept that they must consider the situation at the time the TEN is applied for and cannot take any change that has occurred before the hearing into account. It is therefore open to a landlord to apply for a TEN, be refused it, and then appeal to the RPT taking steps in the meantime to procure that the property is no longer an HMO (see LON/00AG/HMT/2006/0002).

LACORS has made guidance available regarding TENS on their website at www.lacors.gov.uk/lacors/ContentDetails. aspx?id=16963.

Penalties

Not having a licence is a serious matter. Section 72 sets out the offences that can be committed in relation to HMOs. Where a property is required to be licensed and is not, and where the landlord has no outstanding application for a licence or TEN, then the local authority can prosecute and a fine of up to £20,000 can be imposed. The same penalty applies to the overcrowding of an HMO by permitting more occupiers than the licence allows. Breach of any other licence condition attracts a penalty of £5,000.

Early prosecutions have been aimed at severe and persistent offenders who have ignored repeated letters from local authorities. While fines at the maximum level have been imposed, it seems more common for the fine to be in the order of £5,000 to £15,000. Of course local authorities will also seek a contribution to their costs from the defendant, which will push this figure up.

Section 252 of the Housing Act allows the Secretary of State to increase the level of fines under this section by Statutory Instrument.

Rent Repayment Orders

There is a further penalty that can be imposed on individuals who have failed to gain a licence. Section 73 of the Housing Act allows local authorities and individual occupiers to demand repayment of housing benefit (in the case of the local authority) or rent (in the case of a tenant) paid to a landlord who is in default of his licensing obligation.

This penalty only applies where there is neither a licence, an outstanding application for a licence, nor a TEN or an outstanding application for a TEN, and not where the landlord is guilty of some other HMO-related offence. Section 74(8) limits the amount that can be recovered to that paid within the 12 months preceding the application. This is done by making an application to the Residential Property Tribunal for a Rent Repayment Order (RRO).

In order to seek an RRO the local authority must show that the landlord has committed or been convicted of the offence of having an unlicensed HMO and that he has been in receipt of Housing Benefit payments during that period. The local authority will additionally be required to demonstrate that they have served a notice on the landlord prior to the making of the RRO application, stating:

- that they intend seeking an RRO;
- why they propose to do so;
- the amount of money they seek to recover and how it has been calculated; and
- inviting representations within a specified period of not less than 28 days.

Naturally the local authority is not permitted to make its application for an RRO until the 28-day period has ended and until it has properly considered any representations made.

Occupiers do not have to serve notice, but they do need the landlord to have been convicted of the offence of running an unlicensed HMO or for the local authority to have already gained an RRO, for the return of Housing Benefit payments. Therefore tenants are utterly reliant on the local authority prosecuting defaulting landlords or bringing their own private prosecution. They will need to demonstrate:

- that a conviction or RRO has been made;

- that payments were made by the occupier during the time an offence was being committed; and
- that the conviction or previous RRO was made within the preceding 12 months of the occupier's application.

It is important that occupiers are able to clearly show that a conviction or RRO has been made. In CHI/00HH/HMA/2007/0002 the occupier was unable to demonstrate this key point and the local authority officer who accompanied the occupier (presumably to assist him!) confirmed to the tribunal that no prosecution or RRO had been sought by the authority. The occupier's application for an RRO accordingly failed.

It is always necessary for the RPT to consider how much of the money paid it is reasonable to order the landlord to pay back. Where the application is made by a local authority and the landlord has been convicted of the offence of not holding a licence, then the RPT must order that the whole sum of Housing Benefit payments be paid back, but they cannot order that the payment exceed the amount of money actually received by the landlord and they must also consider any exceptional circumstances that would make it unreasonable to order that the whole sum be returned. Where the application is made by an occupier or there has been no conviction for not having a licence, the RPT must consider:

- the total amount paid during the period when the property was unlawfully unlicensed;
- how much of that total was derived from housing benefit and how much was actually received;
- whether there has been a conviction for not having a licence;
- the conduct and financial circumstances of the landlord; and
- where the occupier is making the application, their conduct.

In LON/00BB/HSR/2007/0001 the RPT considered the nature of the burden of proof required when making an RRO for a local authority where a conviction had not already been sought. They accepted that the burden of proof should be analogous to that required in a criminal case in order to prevent local authorities avoiding convictions in cases where their evidence was weak. They noted that this was a problem as, although the Housing Act allows for regulations to require evidence before RPTs to be made on oath, this provision has not been enacted. Ultimately the RPT decided that they should apply the higher criminal standard with respect to demonstrating that an offence had been committed and the amount of benefit that had been paid, but that they could apply the lower civil standard of the balance of probabilities in respect of the notice to the landlord and the amount of benefit that it was reasonable to demand was returned. On this basis they found that the authority had not sufficiently demonstrated that an offence had been committed during the entire period they were seeking an RRO for and their claim was accordingly reduced. It is therefore important for local authorities to make their case thoroughly when seeking an RRO, especially where no previous conviction has occurred.

Restrictions on possession

Under ss. 75 and 98 of the Housing Act, a s. 254 HMO or a property subject to selective licensing that does not have a licence (or for which there is no TEN, or outstanding application for a licence or TEN) is subject to a further penalty above and beyond the financial penalties described above.

This is that no notice pursuant to s. 21 of the *Housing Act* 1988 (as amended) can be served to recover occupation of the property. This prevents landlords from simply stopping properties being HMOs by using the s. 21 notice provisions to remove tenants from the property. Note that no notice can be given during this period. It is not therefore possible to give a notice while the property is unlicensed and then gain a licence thereby validating the notice. A new notice will need to be issued once the licence has been gained.

There is a significant flaw in this provision, however. The definition of unlicensed HMO is as given in ss. 73 and 96 of the Housing Act. This definition is such that any property on which a licence application has been made or one on which a negative decision has been made but the time for appeal for which has not yet passed, or where an appeal has been made and a decision on it is pending, is classed as still licensed for the purposes of this provision. In other words, a landlord could make an application for a licence, **even knowing that the application has no chance of success**, and then issue a s. 21 notice while that application is being considered. In fact the landlord can issue the notice at any time in the 28 days after the application has been rejected, being the time limit for an appeal, or if an appeal has been made but not yet heard. This flaw effectively makes this provision redundant as a landlord could simply file the necessary forms with the local authority without bothering to enclose a fee and then assert that the necessary application had been made and that the notice was therefore effective.

A similar restriction on s. 21 Notices applies in respect of s. 257 HMOs. This was introduced by way of a modification to s. 75 of the Housing Act made by SI 2007/1904 (SI 2007/3231 for Wales). Under the new version of the section the person having control of a s. 257 HMO is prohibited from serving a s. 21 notice on a property inside that HMO. Note that this only applies to the individual who actually controls the HMO. Therefore a freehold owner of a block which is a s. 257 HMO would be unable to serve s. 21 notices in respect of assured shorthold tenancies of flats he controlled within that block. However, a leaseholder of a flat within a block which was a s. 257 HMO would not be prevented from serving a s. 21 notice on his assured shorthold tenant by the failure of his head landlord to secure a s. 257 HMO licence.

4

Management of HMOs

All HMOs are subject to required standards of management, irrespective of whether they require licensing or not. The standards for s. 254 HMOs were set out by SI 2006/372 (SI 2006/1713 (W.175) in Wales). Further standards have now been set out in respect of s. 257 HMOs by SI 2007/1903 (SI 2007/3229 in Wales).

Management of s. 254 HMOs

The requirements for the management of s. 254 HMOs are the same in both England and Wales. They impose duties on both managers and occupiers. The duties are clearly set out in the regulations, and are summarised here.

Managers' duties

Managers must:

- provide their name, address and any telephone number to each household in the HMO and clearly display them in the HMO;
- keep all means of escape from fire in the HMO maintained and unobstructed;
- keep any fire fighting equipment and fire alarms in good working order;
- (where the HMO has five or more occupiers) ensure that all notices indicating the location of means of escape from fire are clearly visible;
- take such measures as are reasonably required to protect the occupiers of the HMO from injury, particularly ensuring that balconies and roofs are safe and that ground-floor windows have adequate accident protection;

- ensure that the water supply and drainage system serving the HMO is maintained in good, clean and working condition and particularly that:
- water tanks are kept in a good, clean and working condition with a cover;
- any water fitting which is liable to damage by frost is protected from frost damage (this excludes overflow pipes or the main supply pipe);
- not unreasonably cause or permit the water or drainage supply that is used by any occupier at the HMO to be interrupted;
- within seven days of receiving a written request from the local authority supply a copy of the gas appliance test certificate;
- ensure that the fixed electrical wiring is inspected and tested at least every five years, obtain a certificate of that test, specifying the results of the test, and supply it to the local authority within seven days of receiving a written request;
- not unreasonably cause the gas or electricity supply that is used by any occupier within the HMO to be interrupted;
- ensure that all common parts of the HMO are maintained in good repair, a safe condition, and kept clear from obstruction;
- ensure that each unit of living accommodation within the HMO and any furniture supplied with it is in clean condition at the beginning of a person's occupation of it;
- ensure that any areas used as living accommodation and any fixtures, fittings, and windows in them are maintained in good repair;
- ensure that sufficient rubbish bins are provided which are adequate for the requirements of each household occupying the HMO for the storage of refuse and litter pending their disposal and make such further arrangements for the disposal of refuse as may be necessary, having regard to any service for such disposal provided by the local authority.

Occupiers

Occupiers must:

- not hinder or frustrate the manager in the performance of his duties under the regulations;
- allow the manager to enter any living accommodation or other place occupied by the occupier at reasonable times where he is carrying out his duties;

- provide the manager, on request, with any such information as he may reasonably require for the purpose of carrying out his duties;
- take reasonable care to avoid causing damage to anything which the manager is under a duty to supply, maintain or repair under the regulations;
- store and dispose of litter in accordance with the arrangements made by the manager; and
- comply with the reasonable instructions of the manager in respect of any means of escape from fire, the prevention of fire and the use of fire equipment.

There is a serious flaw in the regulations. Regulation 11 states:

'**11.** —(1) Nothing in these Regulations shall—

(a)   require or authorise anything to be done in connection with the water supply or drainage or the supply of gas or electricity otherwise than in accordance with any enactment; or

(b)   oblige the manager to take, in connection with those matters, any action which is the responsibility of a local authority or any other person, other than such action as may be necessary to bring the matter promptly to the attention of the authority or person concerned.'

This conflicts with reg. 6(3), which requires that fixed electrical installations are inspected and tested at least every five years. There is no other piece of legislation outside the regulations which imposes such a requirement. How this is to be interpreted is unclear at this time, but there is potential for a challenge to any local authority which seeks to enforce such a requirement.

There are significant duties imposed on managers under these regulations. They should not be ignored, as failure to fulfil the duties is an offence punishable by a fine (currently of up to £5,000). The occupier's duties are less onerous but still significant and attract the same penalties if they are breached. It is important to note that a number of issues that would normally attract a civil liability, such as failure to repair the property, attract a criminal liability by virtue of the management regulations.

Management of s. 257 HMOs

As with s. 254 HMOs, there are management regulations for s. 257 HMOs. Again, they are the same in both England and Wales and apply equally to licensable and non-licensable properties. As before, duties are imposed on both managers and occupiers. The occupiers' duties are exactly the same as those imposed for s. 254 HMOs.

The managers' duties are very similar but they have crucial caveats. In respect of s. 257 HMOs, managers' duties only apply 'in relation to such parts of the HMO over which it would be reasonable to expect the licence holder, in all the circumstances, to exercise control'. The manager cannot be obliged to take 'any action which is the responsibility of a local authority or any other person, other than such action as may be necessary to bring the matter promptly to the attention of the authority or person concerned'. The manager must:

- ensure that his name, address and any telephone contact number are clearly displayed in a prominent position in the common parts of the HMO;
- keep all means of escape from fire in the HMO maintained and unobstructed;
- keep any fire fighting equipment and fire alarms in good working order;
- ensure that all notices indicating the location of means of escape from fire are clearly visible;
- take such measures as are reasonably required to protect the occupiers of the HMO from injury, particularly ensuring that balconies and roofs are safe and that ground-floor windows have adequate accident protection;
- ensure that the water supply and drainage system serving the HMO is maintained in good, clean and working condition and particularly that:
- water tanks are kept in a good, clean and working condition with a cover;
- any water fitting which is liable to damage by frost is protected from frost damage (this excludes overflow pipes or the main supply pipe);
- not unreasonably cause or permit the water or drainage supply that is used by any occupier at the HMO to be interrupted;
- within seven days of receiving a written request from the local authority supply a copy of the gas appliance test certificate;

- ensure that the fixed electrical wiring is inspected and tested at least every five years, obtain a certificate of that test, specifying the results, and supply it to the local authority within seven days of receiving a written request;
- not unreasonably cause the gas or electricity supply that is used by any occupier within the HMO to be interrupted;
- ensure that all common parts of the HMO are maintained in good repair, a safe condition, and kept clear from obstruction, and particularly that handrails, banisters, stair coverings, windows and ventilation are kept in good repair and that the common parts are adequately lit;
- ensure that any areas used as living accommodation and any fixtures, fittings, and windows in them are maintained in good repair subject to the caveat that he is not responsible for disrepair caused by misuse by the occupier of the living accommodation;
- ensure that sufficient bins are provided which are adequate for the requirements of each household occupying the HMO for the storage of refuse and litter pending their disposal and make such further arrangements for the disposal of refuse as may be necessary, having regard to any service for such disposal provided by the local authority;
- ensure that outbuildings, yards and forecourts kept clean and in good repair;
- ensure that any garden belonging to the HMO is kept in a safe and tidy condition;
- ensure that boundary walls, fences and railings of the HMO, are kept and maintained in good and safe repair; and
- ensure that any parts not in use, including any access to them, are kept reasonably clean and free from refuse.

The same problem with these regulations occurs as with the regulations for s. 254 HMOs in respect of the conflict between the requirement to provide an electrical inspection report every five years and the statement that the regulations do not require anything extra to be done beyond that laid out in other legislation.

Just as with the management regulations for s. 254 HMOs, a breach of the regulations is punishable by a fine (currently a maximum of £5,000).

The introduction of management regulations for s. 257 HMOs is of vital interest to block managing agents as they may not always be aware of whether or not individual flats within the blocks they manage are rented out. Many leaseholders will sub-let their flats on short residential leases without bothering to inform their head landlord, due to either ignorance, laziness, or a desire to avoid paying charges levied by their head landlord for consenting to such a lease.

In the past, many head landlords were fairly tolerant of such practices as long as neither they nor other residents were inconvenienced. However, the definition of a s. 257 HMO and the management obligations relating to these mean that such an attitude cannot continue. Head landlords of blocks that have the potential to be s. 257 HMOs will need to be acutely aware of how their long leaseholders are using their properties, as if more than one-third of them are rented on short leases the block will immediately become a s. 257 HMO and the management regulations for s. 257 HMOs will apply. Head landlords that do not pay attention to this could suddenly find themselves in breach of the regulations and subject to criminal penalties, or being asked to carry out works for which they have not budgeted, in order to come into line with the regulations. Head landlords should require (if they are able) leaseholders to ask head landlords for permission to sub-let on short leases, and such permission may well be refused if it will lead to the block being classified as a s. 257 HMO, or permission may be conditional on substantial payment to the head landlord to enable them to ensure the block complies with the regulations.

Who is the manager?

Section 263 of the Housing Act defines the terms 'person having control' and 'person managing'.

- The 'person having control' means the person who receives at least two-thirds of the rent directly from the tenant. This could be either the landlord or the agent.
- The 'person managing' means the person who is the owner or long-leaseholder of the premises, who would or should receive the rent either directly or through and agent.

Codes of practice

Under s. 233 of the *Housing Act* 2004, the government may approve a code of practice for the management of an HMO, although they have not done so at this stage. They will need to have some form of consultation before doing so. Failure to follow such a code will not, in itself, be an offence, but it will, as always, be indicative of poor practice.

Part 3
Control Provisions

5

Control Orders: an overview

What new powers to control housing does the local housing authority have?

The Housing Act 2004 has given local housing authorities (LHAs) new management powers permitting them, by order, to take control of a house or dwelling that has either been unoccupied for at least six months, or is being poorly managed by a landlord. Those orders will be collectively referred to as 'Control Orders'. This chapter will present an overview of Control Orders, while the following chapters will look in turn at: when an order may or should be made; what procedure the LHA must use; and the effect of the making of an order.

The Act also gives LHAs the power to serve 'Overcrowding Notices' to control overcrowding in HMOs that are not covered by the HMO licensing system. Overcrowding Notices will be discussed in Chapter 9.

Types of Control Order

- Interim Management Orders (IMO)
- Final Management Orders (FMO)
- Special Interim Management Orders (SIMO – a variant of the Interim Management Order for use in cases of nuisance)
- Interim Empty Dwelling Management Orders
- Final Empty Dwelling Management Orders

The various Control Orders apply to different kinds of property and have different purposes.

- Management Orders (IMOs and FMOs) deal with homes that are required to be licensed under either Part 2 of the Act (HMO licensing) or Part 3 (selective residential licensing) but are not. These include homes where a local authority has revoked their licence but the revocation is not yet in force.

- In certain circumstances – at present relating solely to anti-social behaviour – a house that would not otherwise require a licence may be subject to a 'Special Interim Management Order' (SIMO).
- The aim of both IMOs, SIMOs and FMOs is to ensure that a property is properly managed.
- Empty Dwelling Management Orders (EDMOs) apply to dwellings that have been unoccupied for at least six months and which do not fall into one of a long list of prescribed exceptions. (For the full list, see Appendix E.)
- The aim of an EDMO is to bring an otherwise empty home back into permanent use.

Confusingly, SIMOs are treated as a variety of IMO by the Act, but they are made in quite different circumstances to an IMO.

In this work they will be treated as different forms of Control Order; accordingly, 'IMO' never includes an 'SIMO'.

Key Differences – Management Orders and EDMOs

- Management Orders apply to buildings; EDMOs apply to dwellings.
- In some circumstances the authority will be under a mandatory duty to make a Management Order; an EDMO is always discretionary.
- The authority may ask an RPT to terminate leases and licences under an EDMO under the *Housing Act* 2004, Sch. 7 para. 22.
- If there is a shortfall between the amount the authority has raised and the amount the authority has spent in respect of the property, under a Management Order this shortfall may be recovered from the immediate landlord in full; under an EDMO, the authority has more limited powers of recovery.

What do the Control Orders do?

Each of the varieties of Control Order transfers the management of a property to the LHA. In the case of IMOs, SIMOs and FMOs, which only apply to rented property, the person displaced will be the immediate landlord; in the case of EDMOs it will be the most appropriate owner of the property (known as the 'relevant proprietor') who is displaced (for a definition of both these concepts see Chapter 8).

The authority may then manage the property and do anything in relation to the property which could or should have been done by the immediate landlord or relevant proprietor, such as:

- receiving rent;
- carrying out repairs;
- creating a new tenancy (in the case of an interim order, only with the written permission of the immediate landlord or relevant proprietor).

It also allows the authority to spend money collected as rent on repairs and on any other 'relevant expenditure'.

Interim and final orders

Control Orders are generally made in two stages. First the LHA will make an interim order, which will ordinarily last up to 12 months. An interim order may then be followed by a series of final orders which will last up to five years (in the case of an FMO) or seven years (in the case of a final EDMO). An SIMO (as the name suggests) will only occur as an interim order and will never be continued by a final order.

The thinking behind this scheme is that an interim order may be sufficient to deal with whatever problems induced the making of the order, but if it is not, a longer-term solution (a final order) will be needed. This is reflected in the fact that the rules for dealing with management and finances under an interim order are dealt with by statute (see Chapter 8), whereas an LHA must draw up a *management scheme* to govern the conduct of a final order.

One significant difference between an interim and a final order is that the LHA may only rent out the property under an interim order with the written permission of a specified person – usually the person who would otherwise be able to let or license the property.

It may well be in the specified person's interest for the property to be rented out, and they may suffer a financial penalty if they refuse (see Chapter 8).

In most other respects, interim and final orders operate in the same way. Any differences will be noted in the following chapters.

Key differences – interim and final orders

- Final orders may only be made if an interim order has first been made.
- Interim orders ordinarily last up to 12 months; final orders my last five or seven years.
- LHA has greater power to rent out the property under a final order.
- Final orders are governed by a *management scheme*.

6

Management Orders: the principles

This chapter deals with the conditions under which an LHA may – or in some cases must – make a Control Order. For each of these, IMO, FMO, SIMO or EDMO, a different set of circumstances applies.

When can an authority make an IMO?

In certain circumstances an authority **may** make an Interim Management Order. In other circumstances it **must** make an order.

Circumstances in which an authority must make an IMO

Where a house which would be required to be licensed under either Part 2 (HMO licensing) or Part 3 (selective residential licensing) of the Act but is not so licensed, the authority has a mandatory duty to make an IMO in one of two situations:

- there is no reasonable prospect of the property becoming licensed in the near future; or
- the 'health and safety condition' (see page 91) test is met (*Housing Act* 2004 s. 102(2)).

A house does not need to be licensed while a temporary exemption notice issued by the authority (issued under *Housing Act* 2004 s. 62 (HMO licensing) or *Housing Act* 2004 s. 86 (selective residential licensing)) is in force.

Where the local housing authority revokes a licence for a house, but while the licence is still in effect because the revocation has not yet taken effect, they may be under a duty to make an IMO in the same circumstances as if the house were not licensed. That is where either:

- there is no reasonable prospect of the property becoming licensed in the near future after the revocation comes into effect; or
- the 'health and safety condition' test will be met when the revocation takes effect (*Housing Act* 2004 s. 102(3).).

Example

A landlord owns an HMO which is unlicensed. He makes an application to the local housing authority for a licence. On receiving his application, the authority think it is very unlikely that they will grant the licence. In these circumstances the authority must make an Interim Management Order.

Even though the landlord is not committing a criminal offence for running an unlicensed HMO (the fact that an application is pending would be a defence), the house will still 'require to be licensed' for the purposes of s. 102 of the Act. If the authority think there is no reasonable prospect of granting the licence, they must make an IMO.

The situation would be the same for a landlord who had applied for a temporary exemption notice which had not yet been refused by the local housing authority. The landlord does not commit an offence, but the house still requires to be licensed.

Circumstances in which an authority may make an IMO

The local housing authority has a discretionary power to make an IMO where:

- the house is an HMO;
- the HMO would not require to be licensed; and
- the 'health and safety condition' is met.

The authority may only make an IMO with the permission of an RPT. In deciding whether to make an IMO in these circumstances the RPT must have regard to the extent to which any applicable code of practice approved under s. 233 has been complied with in respect of the HMO in the past (*Housing Act* 2004 s. 102(4)).

Strictly speaking, there is another circumstance where the authority has a power and not a duty to make an IMO – that is in the case of an SIMO, but for clarity's sake that is being treated as a wholly different kind of order.

The health and safety condition

The health and safety condition is that 'the making of an Interim Management Order is necessary for the purpose of protecting the health, safety or welfare of persons occupying the house, or persons occupying or having an estate or interest in any premises in the vicinity.' (*Housing Act* 2004 s. 104(2)).

Notice that this provision focuses on neighbours as well as those living in a house, so a local authority might make an IMO in order to try to evict nuisance tenants where in their view a landlord is unable or unwilling to do so.

Q: Can the local authority make an IMO against a squat where the squatters are causing nuisance to neighbours?

A: No. A squat would not normally be an HMO (since no consideration is paid for its occupation – see Chapter 2), nor could it require licensing under Part III (which applies only to houses let under a lease or licence); hence no IMO could be made.

Q: What happens if a landlord threatens to evict or indeed actually evicts a tenant in order to avoid licensing?

A: The Act specifically addresses the situation of a landlord who wishes to reduce the number of occupiers of an HMO so that it will not require compulsory licensing. A landlord of an HMO might be tempted to evict sufficient tenants or licensees to avoid having to license a house.

A threat to evict persons occupying a house in order to avoid it having to be licensed under Part 2 of the Act is expressly stated to be capable of being a threat to the welfare of its occupiers (*Housing Act* 2004 s. 103(4)). If a local authority were to decide that it constituted a threat to the health, safety or welfare of the occupiers – which in many cases it might – it would then have a duty to make an IMO.

Houses with HHSRS hazards

It will often be the case that the reason for there being a breach of the health and safety condition is that there are one or more hazards (as defined by the HHSRS) within the property. If there are, it may be that it would be more appropriate for the authority to take enforcement action under the HHSRS, rather than by using an IMO.

Where the local authority would ordinarily have a duty to make an IMO – in other words where a house ought either to be licensed under Parts 2 or 3 or where the authority are seeking to revoke an existing license – the health and safety condition will be treated as **not** being satisfied (and hence the authority will not be required to make an order) if (under *Housing Act 2004* s. 104(4)-(6)):

- the authority is under a duty to take enforcement action because there is a category 1 hazard present in the property (or where the property is licensed and a revocation order has been made but not yet come into force, where the authority would be under such a duty when the revocation order does come into force); and
- the authority considers that the taking of the enforcement action would adequately protect the health, safety or welfare of the persons in question.

When can an authority make an FMO?

As with IMOs, in certain circumstances an authority **may** make an FMO on the expiry of an IMO, and in other circumstances it **must** make an order. These circumstances mirror those for making IMOs, but where the problem is likely to persist long-term after the end of an IMO or FMO.

Circumstances in which an FMO must be made

If, during an IMO or FMO, an LHA considers it will be unable to grant a licence to a house which requires licensing under either Part 2 (HMO licensing) or Part 3 (selective residential licensing), it must make a Final Management Order to take effect on the expiry of the existing order.

Q: My property (an unlicensed HMO) is subject to an IMO which has nearly come to an end. I intend to do work to the property which will mean that it ceases to be an HMO. Can I prevent the authority from making an FMO?

A: No. The Act does not make an exception for a property that will cease to require licensing in the near future. If you apply for a temporary exemption notice (in order to do the work) the authority may then agree to revoke the existing order (or the FMO if it has come into force, see page 105.

Circumstances in which an FMO may be made

Where a house will not require licensing under either Part 2 or Part 3, an authority may still make a Final Management Order at the expiry of an IMO, if it considers this necessary in order to protect, on a long-term basis, the health, safety or welfare of the occupants of the house, or persons occupying or having an estate or interest in any premises in the vicinity.

Special Interim Management Orders (SIMOs)

Part III of the *Housing Act* 2004 permits a local authority to designate areas within its district to be subject to selective residential licensing. There are, at present, two triggers permitting designation: where the area is subject to persistent nuisance or anti-social behaviour; and where there is low housing demand in the area.

The Act recognises that these problems could exist for a single house, when it would not be appropriate to use selective residential licensing as a way to control the problem. The Act permits regulations to be made to permit an SIMO to be made in circumstances analogous to those that trigger the power to designate an area under Part III of the Act.

At present, the regulations in both England and Wales permit an SIMO to be made only in cases where nuisance is caused by a tenant or licensee of a house and the landlord (or licensor) is unable or unwilling to take action to prevent it.

When may a local authority make an SIMO?

An LHA may only make an SIMO with the permission of an RPT. Two sets of conditions apply. The first set of conditions is that:

- the whole of the house must be occupied under a lease or licence of the whole house, or under two or more leases or licences of distinct dwellings that are contained in it (*Housing Act* 2004 s. 103(1));
- none of which was granted by a social landlord (*Housing Act* 2004 s. 79(3) as applied by *Housing Act* 2004 s. 103(1)); and

- none of which would be exempted from licensing under Part 3 by an order made under s. 79(4) of the *Housing Act* 2004. (Note: these exceptions are set out in the Appendix.)

Q: The neighbours of one of my properties own their own home, but are extremely anti-social and this is making it difficult for me to let my property. Can the local authority make an SIMO to assist me?

A: No. An SIMO can only be made where a property is occupied under a lease or licence. The local authority may be able to assist (for example by the use of an anti-social behaviour order), but not under the *Housing Act* 2004.

Q: I have a lodger whom the council say is causing a nuisance to my neighbours. I think the problem is caused by the neighbours, not my lodger, but the council believe them and are threatening to make an SIMO. Can they do that?

A: If you own your home, they cannot make an SIMO. The whole of the property and not just a part of it needs to be rented out.

The second set of conditions are those prescribed for the making of an SIMO:

Prescribed circumstances for making an SIMO

Both the Secretary of State and the Welsh Assembly have prescribed the following identical circumstances for making an SIMO (under the *Housing (Interim Management Orders)(Prescribed Circumstances)(Wales) Order* 2006 (SI 2006/1706) (W.168) and the *Housing (Interim Management Orders)(Prescribed Circumstances)(England) Order 2006* (SI 2006/369)):

- the area in which the house is located is experiencing a significant and persistent problem caused by anti-social behaviour;
- that problem is attributable, in whole or in part, to the anti-social behaviour of an occupier of the house;
- the landlord of the house is a private sector landlord (the term 'private sector landlord' does not include a registered social landlord within the meaning of Part 1 of the *Housing Act* 1996);
- the landlord of the house is failing to take the appropriate action to combat that problem;
- the making of an Interim Management Order, when combined with other measures taken in the area by the local housing authority, or by other persons together with the local housing authority, will lead to a reduction in, or elimination of, that problem.

Authorisation of an SIMO by the RPT

An SIMO is never mandatory, so an authority requires the authorisation of the RPT before making an SIMO (*Housing Act* 2004 s. 103(7)). An RPT may only authorise the making of an SIMO where:

- the house meets the prescribed conditions given above; and
- the order is necessary for the purpose of protecting the health, safety or welfare of persons occupying, visiting or otherwise engaging in lawful activities in the vicinity of the house (*Housing Act* 2004 s. 103(4)).

The second condition may look like the 'health and safety condition' for making certain IMOs, but it is much wider. An SIMO can be made to protect innocent passers-by or users of nearby facilities as well as those who live near an offending property. The 'health and safety condition' is restricted to considering those living in the neighbourhood or those with an interest in nearby property.

When can an authority make an Interim Empty Dwelling Management Order (EDMO)?

An EDMO is always discretionary and therefore always requires the authorisation of an RPT. EDMOs may only be made for certain kinds of property and only in certain circumstances.

Property which may be the subject of an EDMO

As the name suggests, EDMOs apply to 'dwellings'. For the purposes of making an EDMO, the law distinguishes between two kinds of dwelling (*Housing Act* 2004 s. 134(4)(a)):

- a building intended to be occupied as a separate dwelling; or
- a part of a building intended to be occupied as a separate dwelling which may be entered otherwise than through any non-residential accommodation in the building.

Most flats intended to be occupied as a separate dwelling will be dwellings for the purposes of the making of an EDMO.

> **Q: What happens if I own a shop with a flat above, and the flat remains empty? Will the flat be classed as an 'empty dwelling'?**
>
> **A:** If access to the flat is through the shop, it cannot be classed as a separate dwelling or made the subject of an EDMO. If, on the other hand, the flat has its own separate access, independent of the shop, it is classed as a separate dwelling.

Where an EDMO refers to 'the dwelling', it is referring to the dwelling for which the EDMO is made; there is no need for the order itself to explicitly recite a definition (*Housing Act* 2004 s. 134(4)(b)).

Presumably, the word 'dwelling' will be interpreted in accordance with existing case law on the interpretation of the phrase 'as a separate dwelling' used in the Rent Acts and the *Housing Act* 1988, which has established that even a hotel room equipped with rudimentary cooking equipment is capable of being a separate dwelling (*Uratemp Ventures Ltd v Collins* [2001] UKHL 43; [2001] 3 WLR 806).

Conditions for making an interim EDMO

A local housing authority may make an interim EDMO provided that:

- the dwelling is wholly unoccupied;
- the relevant proprietor is not a public sector body;
- they receive authorisation from an RPT to do so.

The RPT will require further conditions to be satisfied before it authorises the authority to make an interim EDMO (for which see page 101). The most relevant to note here is that the property will have to have been wholly unoccupied for at least six months, which would exclude temporary voids in the letting of a property. There is also a list of exceptions – such as owner occupation – which prevent the making of an interim EDMO (see Appendix E for a full list).

Here 'wholly unoccupied' means that no part is occupied, whether lawfully or unlawfully.

> **Example**
>
> If a large house is part occupied by squatters but otherwise empty, the local housing authority will not be able to make an interim EDMO for the remainder of the house unless it is a part that is intended to be occupied as a separate dwelling.

Conditions for making a final EDMO

A final EDMO may replace either an interim EDMO or a final EDMO. As with an interim EDMO the authority always has a discretion as to whether to make a final EDMO. It may do so if the following conditions are satisfied:

- unless a final EDMO is made, the dwelling is likely to become or remain unoccupied;
- if the dwelling is unoccupied, they have taken such steps as it was appropriate for them to take under the existing EDMO with a view to securing the occupation of the dwelling.

> **Example**
>
> An empty dwelling is subject to an interim EDMO. The authority believe that the dwelling could be usefully let, but the relevant proprietor has refused to give them written permission to do so. The local authority may then make a final EDMO to replace the interim EDMO in order to give them the power to let the property.

7

Control Orders: procedures

Making interim orders – overview

Interim orders are made by the LHA. For an IMO or SIMO, no preliminaries are required before the making of an order, although where the authority has the discretion, rather than an obligation, to make the order, it must first obtain authorisation from the Residential Property Tribunal (RPT).

For an interim EDMO, the authority must first consult with the relevant proprietor and consider any objections they may raise.

The authority then makes the order, which comes into force on the date it is made. The authority then has seven days to notify relevant people that the order has been made.

Procedure for interim orders – summary

- For interim EDMO's only: consult with relevant proprietor.
- If the order is not mandatory: make an application to the RPT.
- RPT authorises the making of the order.
- Authority makes the order.
- Authority notifies relevant people within seven days that the order has been made.

Making an IMO

Where the authority is under a duty to make an IMO, they will do so without further ceremony.

In the case of HMOs which fall outside the licensing scheme, the authority may have a power to make an IMO as discussed in the previous chapter. The authority must first seek the authorisation of the RPT. Details on RPT procedure are given in Chapter 11.

The RPT is not required to give authorisation: even if it finds that the conditions for the exercise of the authority's power are made out, it has a discretion to do so. In exercising that discretion it must have regard to the extent to which any applicable code of practice (for management of HMOs) was complied with in respect of the HMO in the past.

Making an SIMO

The authority will also have to apply to the RPT for authorisation to make an SIMO. The RPT will only make an SIMO if it considers the relevant conditions are met (these are set out in Chapter 5). It appears that an RPT may still have the discretion not to make an order even where all these conditions are met.

Making an EDMO

Interim EDMOs: consultation and notification

The first step in making an interim EDMO is for the authority to consult with the relevant proprietor. The thinking behind the requirement to consult before making an interim EDMO appears to be that an EDMO effectively denies the relevant proprietor, who has acted entirely lawfully, of the use of their property. This contrasts with the situation where an authority makes a mandatory IMO when the immediate landlord has some degree of fault.

It is not entirely clear why a consultation requirement is needed, since the authority will have to apply to an RTP for authorisation to make an EDMO. The RPT will inform the relevant proprietor of the proceedings, who will have an opportunity to respond (*Procedure Regulations*, reg. 7). The authority is required to carry out consultation with the relevant proprietor before making an interim EDMO.

Before deciding whether to make an EDMO, the authority must make all reasonable efforts to notify the relevant proprietor that they are considering making an interim EDMO in respect of the dwelling and to ascertain what steps (if any) the relevant proprietor is taking, or is intending to take, to secure that the dwelling is occupied (s. 133(3)). The RPT will not make an order unless it is satisfied that the authority has complied with this requirement.

The authority must then, when deciding whether to make an application to an RPT for an interim EDMO, take into account the rights of the relevant proprietor of the dwelling and the interests of the wider community (s. 133(4)).

There is no requirement for an RPT to check whether the authority has complied with this requirement and so in principle such a failure could be challenged by judicial review. However, the RPT will have to consider afresh the rights of the relevant proprietor and the interest of the community so judicial review would almost always be inappropriate.

Application to the RPT

The authority may then apply to the RPT. (Details of the application process are given later.) An RPT may not authorise an interim EDMO unless:

- the dwelling has been wholly unoccupied for at least six months;
- there is no reasonable prospect that the dwelling will become occupied in the near future;
- if an interim order is made, there is a reasonable prospect that the dwelling will become occupied;
- the authority have complied with s. 133(3) – that is that it has properly consulted with the relevant proprietor; and
- any prescribed requirements have been complied with.

The RPT must also be satisfied that none of the prescribed exceptions applies. A list of these prescribed exceptions is provided in Appendix E. This sets out a number of circumstances where a property might legitimately be unoccupied.

In deciding whether to authorise an interim EDMO, the RPT must take into account:

- the interests of the community;

- the effect that the order will have on the rights of the relevant proprietor and may have on the rights of third parties.

> **Q: My property was unoccupied for longer than six months and the local authority have made an application to the RPT for an interim EDMO. I have just been able to find tenants for the property, if I put them in, will that stop the EDMO being made?**
>
> **A:** Yes. The RPT considers what the situation is at the date of the hearing, not at the time the local authority were considering making the order.

Compensation

In order to protect the interests of third parties, the RPT may, on authorising an interim EDMO, make an order requiring the authority (if they make the EDMO) to pay to any third party specified in the order an amount of compensation in respect of any interference in consequence of the order with the rights of the third party.

There is no guidance on when such compensation ought to be given.

> **Q: Can a mortgage lender request compensation when an EDMO is made?**
>
> **A:** The answer would seem to be no, if the borrower has continued to maintain their mortgage payments even though the property was unoccupied.
>
> In CAM/38UD/HYI/2006/0001 the property was subject to a mortgage. The RPT refused the mortgage lender's request to order compensation to be paid to them, holding that an order for compensation was not automatic and there was no reason to suppose that the mortgage lender would be financially worse off because of the making of the order – the borrower had been maintaining the payments even though the property was unoccupied.

Coming into force

An interim order comes into force on the date it is made by the authority (Sch. 7 paras 1(2), 105(2)) unless it is an Interim Management Order made in the expectation that an existing licence for the house under Part 2 or Part 3 will be revoked, in which case the coming into force of the order is delayed until the revocation of the licence itself comes itself into force (s. 105(3)).

Making final orders

Under Sch. 6 Part 1, applied to final EDMOs by s. 136(5), the authority must consult with the relevant persons concerned before making a final order. It must serve, on each 'relevant person', a copy of the proposed order, together with a notice setting out:

- the reasons for making the order;
- the main terms of the proposed order including those of the management scheme (see discussion of management schemes);
- the length of the consultation period, during which the relevant person may make representations to the authority about the making of the order.

The authority must then consider any representations made in accordance with the notice which are not withdrawn. If, having considered any representations, the authority propose to make a final order with modifications, they must serve a further notice, setting out:

- the proposed modifications;
- the reasons for them; and
- the length of the consultation period.

This process must be repeated as long as the authority wishes to make further modifications to the order after receiving further representations, although it is to be hoped that the authority will eventually settle on a form of order.

Note that the authority does not need to serve a further notice if it considers that the modifications are not material in any respect or, if further modifications are proposed that these further modifications do not differ in any material respect from the last proposed modifications.

By contrast with the position for interim orders, there is never any need to obtain authorisation from an RPT in order to make a final order. The only remedy of an aggrieved owner or landlord would be to appeal.

If a final EDMO is being made, the RPT must again consider whether compensation should be paid to any third parties.

Notification procedure after an order is made

Once the order has been made (see Sch. 6 paras 7-8 applied to interim EDMOs by s. 133(8) and final EDMOs by s. 136(5)), the authority must within seven days, beginning with the day on which the order is made, serve on each relevant person a copy of the order and a notice which sets out (Sch. 6 paras 7(5)-(7) (relating to Management Orders) applied to EDMOs by ss. 133(8) and 136(5)):

- the reasons for making the order;
- the date on which it was made;
- the general effect of the order;
- the date on which the order will cease to have effect (or in the case of an IMO, to take effect on the revocation of a licence, how that date is to be calculated).

In addition, the notice must inform any relevant persons of their right of appeal against the order and the period (if any) within which any such appeal may be made, and (if it is a final order), a general description of the way in which the house is to be managed by the authority in accordance with the management scheme contained in the order.

There does not appear to be any negative consequence for the authority if it fails to comply with these requirements. The order will have taken effect when it was made in any case, and the authority will have a right of possession. This is worrying, because it appears that there are published standard forms of order that give incorrect information as to the right to appeal. This was a point of comment in CAM/00JA/HY1/2007/0002.

If the authority fails to comply with its service requirements in time, or serves confusing or inaccurate information as to the right of appeal, a prejudiced individual would almost certainly have a good argument for being given an extension of time in which to appeal against the order.

In the case of a Management Order, the authority must also, as soon as practicable after the order has been made, serve the same on any occupiers of the house, although the notice need not set out information as to a right of appeal.

Those documents are to be regarded as having been served on the occupiers if they are fixed to a conspicuous part of the house. Clearly the assumption is that an EDMO will only be made when there are no occupiers of the house and therefore no notice need be served on them. This may cause difficulty where an authority wrongly identifies a dwelling as being empty, as there is no reason why any occupiers should become aware of the order at this stage.

Variation and revocation of an order

During the operation of a final order the authority is under an express duty to review the operation of the order and its management scheme from time to time (s. 115(3) (Management Orders) and s. 137(4) (EDMOs)).

Variations

If, on review, the authority decides that any variations should be made, they must then make those variations (s. 115(4) (Management Orders) and s. 137(5) (EDMOs)). An authority has a general power to vary an order if it considers it appropriate to do so (Sch. 7, paras 6(1), 15(1), ss. 111(1) and 121(1)).

Revocations

The authority is never required to revoke an order, but it has the power, in certain circumstances to do so. In general an order may be revoked where:

- a new order (a final order or a further final order) has been made (Sch. 7, paras 7(1)(c), 16(1)(c), ss. 112(1)(c) and 122(1)(c));
- if in any other circumstances the authority consider it appropriate to revoke the order (Sch. 7, paras 7(1)(e), 16(1)(e), ss. 112(1)(d) and 122(1)(d)) (but, if the property is occupied under an EDMO, the authority may only rely on this ground with the consent of the relevant proprietor) (Sch. 7, paras 7(2), 16(2)).

The last proviso may be intended to prevent an authority taking over an empty property, letting it to tenants and then on finding themselves in difficulty with the management of the property, trying to return the responsibility to the landlord.

IMO, FMO and SIMOs

An IMO, FMO or SIMO may be revoked if:

- it was made under a mandatory ground, but Part 2 and Part 3 of the Act no longer apply to it (ss 112(1)(a) and 122(1)(a));
- it was made under a mandatory ground and a licence is due to come into force for the house from the date of revocation of the order (ss 112(1)(b) and 122(1)(b)).

EDMOs

If an authority concludes that there are no steps it could appropriately take for the purpose of securing that a dwelling is occupied, it must either (s. 135(4) (interim EDMO), s. 137(6)(a) (final EDMO)):

- revoke the order; or
- (in the case of an interim EDMO) consider making a final EDMO.

(Note. The assumption of the second limb is that the authority's greater leasing powers under a final EDMO would make the difference between occupation and non-occupation.)

In addition, if an authority considers that a final EDMO is unnecessary, under s. 137(6)(b) it must revoke the order.

An EDMO may also be revoked – in the case of a property which is occupied, only with the consent of the relevant proprietor – if:

- the dwelling will either become or continue to be occupied, despite the order being revoked;
- the dwelling is to be sold; or
- the authority concludes that it would be appropriate to revoke the order in order to prevent or stop interference with the rights of a third party in consequence of the order.

Procedure for revocation

The authority may vary or revoke an order on its own initiative or on the application of a 'relevant person'.

For the purposes of an IMO, FMO or SIMO, a relevant person is defined in s. 112(4) as:

- any person who has an estate or interest in the house or part of it (but is not a tenant under a lease with an unexpired term of three years or less);
- any other person who (but for the order) would be a person managing or having control of the house or part of it.

For the purposes of an EDMO, a 'relevant person' is any person who has an estate or interest in the dwelling (other than a person who is a tenant under a 'lease' granted under the authority's power to create interest with all the incidents of a leasehold).

There does not appear to be any logical reason for the different definition of 'relevant person' between the two types of order. Obviously anyone may communicate with an authority and ask them to vary or revoke an order, but only a 'relevant person' will be able to exercise a right of appeal.

A variation or revocation comes into force at the 'operative time' – in other words, after the time for appealing has passed – as described for final orders, above.

Expiry of an order

As well as the possibility of being revoked by the authority, all orders have a default period of operation after they are made (even where the coming into force is delayed, in the case of an IMO coming into force on the revocation of a licence). The time span for the expiry of the various types of order is given below.

Time span for the expiry of an order
Interim orders: 12 months (Sch. 7 para. 1(3), s. 105(4))
Final Management Orders: five years (s. 114(4)
Final EDMOs: seven years (Sch. 7 para. 9(3))

Various circumstances can alter the termination date.

In the case of an IMO, the coming into force of which is delayed, under s. 105(6)-(7), the IMO must include a provision stating the date on which it is to cease to have effect; that date may be no more than 12 months after the date on which the order comes into force. The order itself may state an earlier date on which it will come to an end (Sch. 7 paras 1(4), 9(4), ss. 105(5) and 114(4)).

A final EDMO may be extended with the consent of the relevant proprietor, but there appears to be no requirement for that consent to be written (see Sch. 7 para. 9(5)).

An order may be extended if it is due to be replaced by a further order the coming into force of which is delayed by an appeal. If this occurs, the order will normally be extended until the 'operative time', which is calculated as follows:

- where there may be an appeal against the new order, the operative time is 28 days after the making of the order;
- if an appeal is made, the operative time is extended to the date the order is upheld on appeal and either:
- the date for a further appeal to the Lands Tribunal has passed; or
- an appeal is made to the Lands Tribunal and that order upheld.

If an appeal is withdrawn, it is treated as if the appeal has been decided. 'Upholding' an order encompasses the situation where the RPT or Lands Tribunal varies the new order.

The authority may also apply to a tribunal for an order that the existing order remain in effect until the appeal process is completed – a provision the authority are most likely to use where the new order has been overturned by the RPT, but the authority hope that an onward appeal to the Lands Tribunal will be successful.

In the case of Management Orders, there is a further condition for the extension of an existing order pending appeal. The house must:

- require licensing (under either Part 2 or Part 3); and
- the new order, or a new licence or a new IMO (or in the case of an FMO, a temporary exemption notice) will fall after the end of the expiry of the IMO because of the appeal.

This means that IMOs made under the authority's discretionary powers will not normally be extended pending appeal, since they will usually affect houses that do not require licensing.

8

Control Orders: their effect

Effect of an order on occupiers, landlords and proprietors

Once an order is in place the authority will have a right of possession of the property. This right is subject to the rights of 'existing occupiers' being observed. While the order is in force, the authority will take over most of the rights and duties of individuals known as 'immediate landlords' (in the case of a Management Order) or an individual known as the 'relevant proprietor' (in the case of an EDMO).

Who is the 'immediate landlord'?

A person is regarded as the 'immediate landlord' of the whole or a part of a house if they (ss 109(6) (IMOs) and 118(6) (FMOs), combined with the effects of s. 124(4).):

- are the owner or lessee of the house (or part);
- are not themselves an existing occupier; and
- are the lessor or licensor of a lease or licence under which an existing occupier occupies the whole or part of the house.

If there are no existing occupiers, as in examples 1 and 2 given below, there can be no immediate landlord.

Who is the relevant proprietor ?

The 'relevant proprietor' is the person whose rights and obligations will be temporarily replaced by that of the authority during the currency of an EDMO.

- Where a dwelling is let under one or more leases with an unexpired term of seven years or more, the lessee under whichever lease has the shortest unexpired term is the relevant proprietor.
- If the dwelling is not let under a lease with an unexpired term of at least seven years, the relevant proprietor is the freeholder.

Q: Is it possible that the identity of the relevant proprietor might change as time passes?

A: This is quite possible, as where a dwelling is let under one or more leases the identity of the relevant proprietor might change as time goes on. The date on which the identity of the relevant proprietor is to be determined depends on the stage which proceedings have reached, and logically different individuals might be the 'relevant proprietor' at different stages of the process.

Where the authority is considering whether to make an interim EDMO, the identity of the relevant proprietor is determined at the date when the authority first takes steps to consult under s. 133(3) of the Act (s. 132(5)(a)).

Where an interim EDMO has been made, during the operation of an interim EDMO or any subsequent final EDMO, the relevant proprietor is determined at the time the application for authorisation to the RPT was made (s. 132(5)(b)-(c)).

Given that there is no limit to the number of final EDMOs that may be made in succession, it is entirely possible that the relevant proprietor's leasehold interest might have expired before the EDMO comes to an end.

Rights of existing occupiers

Existing occupiers' rights take precedence over the authority's right to possession. In most cases the authority will be treated as if they were the lessor or licensor of any existing occupiers and may have the right to gain possession under that lease or license – for instance, if an existing occupier falls into arrears of rent.

Existing occupiers do not gain additional rights by virtue of the Act.

Existing occupiers are contrasted with 'new occupiers' – someone to whom a 'lease' or 'licence' is granted under the authority's power to grant rights akin to a lease or licence.

Q: In the case of an IMO, FMO or SIMO, who is the existing occupier?

A: Under an IMO, FMO or SIMO, an 'existing occupier' is someone who:
- in the case of an HMO or Part 3 house, is occupying part of the house and does not have an estate or interest in the whole of the house; or
- in the case of a Part 3 house, is occupying the whole of the house.

The reason for the difference in treatment of an HMO and a Part 3 house appears to be that someone who is occupying the whole of an HMO and has an estate or interest in the HMO will be partly responsible for the condition of its management. The thinking may be that the interests of such a person should not be protected, since they are 'at fault' in failing to ensure that the HMO is properly managed.

Whatever the reason for this definition, it gives rise to a number of problems, which the following examples illustrate.

Example 1: SIMOs

An SIMO may be made in respect of a house which is neither an HMO nor a Part 3 house, in which case there will be no 'existing occupiers' whose rights are protected. While at least one occupier of such a house may be guilty of anti-social behaviour, it does not seem clear that Parliament intended that no occupier should be protected in the case of an SIMO.

Example 2: Student joint tenants

A house consisting of three floors and that is let to five or more students on a joint tenancy of the whole of the house – an arrangement common in many university towns – will have no existing occupiers. The property will be an HMO that requires licensing, but the students will have an interest in the whole of the house, not a part of the house, and thus be excluded from being existing occupiers.

Example 3: Owner living with lodgers

Consider a house occupied by two joint owners of the house together with three others who are not related to them. This is a not uncommon arrangement. Yet, the inevitable conclusion is that the two joint owners are not 'existing occupiers' (because they have an interest in the whole of the house).

Who is the existing occupier in the case of an EDMO?

Matters are more straightforward for EDMOs. In the case of an EDMO, an existing occupier is someone, other than the relevant proprietor, who has a right to occupy the dwelling (Sch. 7 para.18(2).

Duties of the local housing authority while the order is in force

A Control Order imposes a number of duties on the local housing authority. As soon as practicable after an interim order has come into force, and as soon as a final order is in force, the authority is required to take such steps as it considers appropriate:

- (under an EDMO) in order to ensure that the property is (and in the case of an interim EDMO, continues to be) occupied (ss 135(2) and 137(2));
- (under an IMO) for protecting the health, safety or welfare of persons occupying the house, or persons occupying or having an estate or interest in any premises in the vicinity (s. 106(2));
- for the proper management of the dwelling:

In the case of an interim order, this will be pending the making of a final EDMO, the revocation of the interim EDMO or, in the case of an IMO, the granting of a licence (s. 135(3)). In the case of a final order, this will be in accordance with the management scheme that forms part of the order (s. 109(2) (a Final Management Order) and s. 137(7) (a final EDMO)).

LHA's duties: finance and insurance

The Act sets out certain requirements relating to finance and insurance.

- It requires an authority to keep full accounts of its income and expenditure in respect of the dwelling.
- It requires an authority to make available to the 'relevant landlord' (in the case of a Management Order) or the 'relevant proprietor' (in the case of an EDMO), and to any other person who has an estate or interest in the dwelling,

all reasonable facilities for inspecting, taking copies of and verifying those accounts (Sch. 7 paras 5(6)(a) and 13(5)(a), ss. 110(6)(a) and 119(7)(a)).

- As part of the proper management of the dwelling, it requires the LHA to insure the property against destruction or damage, in particular by fire (ss 135(5) and 137(7)).

LHA's duties: reviewing the order

Under an FMO the authority must keep the operation of the order and in particular the management scheme, under regular review (s. 115(3) (a Final Management Order) and s. 137(4) (a final EDMO)).

Under an IMO there is no express duty requiring an authority to keep the order under review although some form of monitoring is implicit in the notion of 'appropriate steps' for the proper management of a dwelling.

Powers of the local housing authority

In order to comply with its duties under the order, the authority is given a number of powers during the period for which the order is in force. These are:

- a right to possession subject to existing occupiers (Sch. 7 paras 2(3)(a), 10(3)(a), ss. 107(3)(a) and 116(3)(a));
- a right to do (and authorise a manager or other person to do) all that the relevant proprietor (for EDMOs) or a person with an estate or interest in the house (for Management Orders) would (but for the order) be entitled to do (subject to the exceptions noted below) (Sch. 7 paras 2(3)(b), 10(3)(b), ss. 107(3)(b) and 116(3)(b));
- a right to create an interest similar to a lease or licence of the property (Sch. 7 paras 2(3)(c), 10(3)(c), ss. 107(3)(b) and 116(3)(b)) (in the case of an interim order, only with the written consent of the relevant proprietor and if the relevant proprietor is a lessee, not for a term longer than the remaining term of that lease; in the case of a final order with the written permission of the relevant proprietor, only in certain circumstances);
- a power of entry to carry out works (Sch. 7 para. 25, s. 131).

What the local authority does not acquire is any estate or interest in the property, and so it cannot charge, sell, lease or otherwise dispose of it (Sch. 7 paras 2(5), 10(5)).

Leases and licences

Terminating a lease or licence

Under an EDMO the authority gains an additional right to apply to an RPT for an order terminating a lease or licence (Sch. 7 paras 2(3)(d), 10(3)(d)). The RPT may make such an order if it is satisfied that the dwelling is not being occupied and that the local housing authority needs to have the right to possession of the dwelling in order to secure that the dwelling becomes occupied.

The application may be made in respect of:

- leases for which the relevant proprietor is the lessor;
- any sub lease of such a lease;
- a licence of the dwelling.

Presumably 'licence of the dwelling' includes a licence to occupy any part of the dwelling. The licence need not have been made by the relevant proprietor or any under-tenant.

The RPT may make an order terminating a lease or licence either:

- while an interim or final EDMO is in place; or
- after the authority has successfully applied for permission to make an interim EDMO

In practice, an authority could apply to the RPT for permission to make an interim EDMO and for termination of any lease or licence at the same time.

Creating new leases and licences

As explained above, the authority may not let a property since it is not the legal owner; however it is able to create interests that are treated, in almost all respects, as if they were leases and licences.

The Act empowers the local authority to grant a lease of the whole of the property or a licence of a part of the property; the converse would appear to be impossible. This is odd, because the difference between a lease and a licence is determined primarily by exclusivity of occupation, not the extent of the demised premises.

During the operation of an interim order, the authority must have the written permission of the relevant proprietor in order to create a 'lease' or 'licence'. This restriction is relaxed for the authority during the operation of a final order. A local authority will require the written permission of the relevant proprietor or immediate landlord when:

- the 'lease' or 'licence' is for a fixed term which expires after the order is due to expire; or
- where the 'lease' or 'licence' is terminable by notice to quit or an equivalent notice of more than four weeks.

It would appear that 'terminable by notice to quit' includes a periodic tenancy of any kind, so that a monthly tenancy would require written permission of the relevant proprietor unless it had an explicit clause permitting four weeks' notice only to be given.

Assured shorthold tenancies

An exception to the above rule is made for an assured shorthold tenancy. An authority does not require written permission to create any assured shorthold tenancy, provided it is created more than six months before the final order is due to expire. This is a peculiar exception and appears to be based on the belief that, after six months, a landlord may terminate an assured shorthold tenancy by notice. Of course, this is not true and assured shorthold tenancies for fixed terms of one year or more are commonplace, and those for terms of two or more years are not unknown.

There is also no requirement that an assured shorthold tenancy should have any clause permitting the landlord to regain possession, should the tenant breach any covenant in the lease (such as by failing to pay rent). It is easy to create such a tenancy inadvertently and, coupled with a long fixed term, such a tenancy could permit a tenant to remain in occupation without paying any rent to their landlord. Though it is to be hoped that such a situation will be unusual, it is surprising that the Act does not preclude any such eventuality.

Existing superior leases

Where a superior lease exists, the relevant proprietor or immediate landlords are themselves only lessees. When this is the case the authority is substituted for them as lessee, although it does not acquire an interest in the property. As lessee the authority becomes liable, under the lessee's covenant, for such things as paying rent or service charges.

Existing tenants

Similarly, where:

- (under an EDMO) the relevant proprietor is a lessor or licensor (Sch. 7 paras 4(2), 12(2)); or
- (in the case of a Management Order) where there are existing occupiers who hold from a lessor or licensor who is not themselves an existing occupier (s. 124(4)),

the authority is treated as if they were the lessor or licensor under the lease or licence while the order is in force.

The authority does not gain any estate or interest in the property as a result of being treated as a lessor but the lease is to continue to have effect, as far as possible, as if it were a valid lease between the authority and the lessees (s. 124(5), Sch. 7 paras 4(3), 12(3)).

Statutory housing codes

Normally certain statutory provisions exclude local authority lettings from the operation of various housing codes. These do not have effect where a local authority is treated as if it were lessor or licensor, namely:

- ss. 14 to 16 of the *Rent Act* 1977, which excludes local authority lettings from the operation of the *Rent Act*;
- the same provisions as applied in the *Rent (Agriculture) Act* 1976;
- s. 1(2) of and para. 12 of Sch. 1 to the *Housing Act* 1988, which exclude local authority lettings from being assured tenancies or assured agricultural occupancies.

Where an authority is treated as a lessor or licensor, whether because it has been substituted for a relevant proprietor or immediate landlord, or because it has created a lease under the authority's power to create 'leases' or 'licences', the local authority is not to be treated as the legal owner of the premises for the purposes of:

- s. 80 of the *Housing Act* 1985 (the landlord condition for secure tenancies);
- s. 124 of the *Housing Act* 1996 (concerning introductory tenancies).

So the authority will be able to create and/or take over assured (and assured shorthold) tenancies and will not thereby create a secure or introductory tenancy. Indeed the authority will not be able to create secure tenancies of the premises (s. 124(9)-(10), Sch. 7 paras 4 (5)-(6), 12 (5)-(6) and 18(6)-(7)).

The rights of others under a Control Order

Immediate landlord or relevant proprietor

While a Management Order is in force, the immediate landlord has no right to receive rents or other payments payable to the authority under s. 124(4) or payable to the authority as a result of the creation of rights akin to 'leases' and 'licences' by the authority (ss 109(2)(a) and 118(2)(a)). This would appear to mean that the immediate landlord would be entitled to recover sums not attributable to either of these heads, for example where a trespasser must pay an occupation charge, although that surely cannot be the intention of the legislation.

The rule is expressed more clearly under an EDMO where the relevant proprietor is not permitted to recover any sum that is payment for occupation of the property (Sch. 7 paras 4(7)(a) and 12(7)(a)).

The relevant proprietor or immediate landlord:

- may not exercise any rights or powers of management of the dwelling;
- may not create any leasehold interest in the dwelling (other than a lease of the reversion) or any licence or other right to occupy the dwelling.

But the relevant proprietor, or anyone else having an estate or interest in the dwelling, is free to make any disposition of that estate or interest, which will include selling or mortgaging it (Sch. 7, paras 4(8) and 12(8) and ss. 109(3) and 118(3)).

Mortgagees and lessors

The rights of and remedies available to any mortgagee of the house or dwelling and any lease of the house or dwelling, under which the relevant proprietor or relevant landlord is a lessor (or under-lessor) are unaffected by an order, except to the extent that any of those rights or remedies would prevent the authority carrying out its duties (Sch. 7, paras 4(9) and 12(9) and ss. 109(4) and 118(4)).

In proceedings for the enforcement of any such rights or remedies a court may make such order as it thinks fit as regards the operation of the order (including an order quashing it) (Sch. 7, paras 4(10) and 12(10) and ss. 109(5) and 118(5)). For example, where a mortgagee wishes to exercise a power of sale, a court could quash an EDMO so that the mortgagee may regain possession.

Financial arrangements

Interim orders

During the operation of an interim order, the authority is permitted to receive rent and spend it or any other payment it has collected on:

- 'relevant expenditure';
- compensation to third parties ordered by an RPT (Sch. 7 para. 5(3) and s. 110(3)).

What counts as 'relevant expenditure'?

Relevant expenditure means any expenditure reasonably incurred by the authority in the carrying out of its duties (Sch. 7, para. 5(2)(b) and s. 110(2)). In the case of an EDMO, 'relevant expenditure' also includes any expenditure incurred with the consent of the relevant proprietor in the carrying out of its duties (Sch. 7, para. 5(2)(a)). This provision means that, under an interim EDMO, the authority may agree with the relevant proprietor to incur expenditure without being concerned that the amount might later be found to be unreasonable.

The authority must pay to the relevant proprietor (in the case of an EDMO) or the 'relevant landlord' – the immediately superior landlord of the property or any part of it (s. 110(8)) – in the case of a Management Order:

- any sums remaining from rent and other payments after the amount spent by the authority on relevant expenditure and compensation to third parties has been deducted;
- interest.

The authority may decide on the rate of interest it considers appropriate and the intervals between payments. The interim order may, but is not required to, make provision for the rates of interest and the intervals between payments. There appears to be no express requirement that any sums should be paid before the end of the order, although it is to be hoped that the authority would make more regular payments to an immediate landlord or relevant proprietor.

Management schemes and FMOs

The financial arrangements that operate during a final order are governed by a 'management scheme'. This sets out in detail the way in which the management of the house or dwelling will be organised. The management scheme in a final order is of great importance to the immediate landlord or relevant proprietor and to others connected with the property, as it sets out their rights and, in some cases, liabilities.

The terms of the management scheme may be appealed to the RPT (Sch. 6, para. 24(1) (FMOs) and Sch. 7, para. 26(1) (final EDMOs)). Such a challenge is normally only possible within 28 days of the making of the final order, so those affected by the order should scrutinise the order carefully from the outset. In proceedings for the enforcement of a management scheme, which are dealt with on page 121, the RPT may vary or revoke the terms of the management scheme.

Under an FMO, the management scheme is divided into two parts. Part 1 of an FMO management scheme has a very similar structure to the whole of a management scheme made under a final EDMO. Both must specify the following (s. 119(4) (FMOs) and Sch. 7, para. 13(3) (for a final EDMO)):

- Details of any works that the LHA intends to carry out in connection with the house or dwelling.

- An estimate of the capital and other expenditure to be incurred by the authority in respect of the house or dwelling while the order is in force.
- The amount of rent or other payments that the LHA will seek to obtain. Under an FMO the authority is required to have regard to the condition or expected condition of the house at any time while the order is in force. (An odd requirement, since it would probably be irrational for the authority not to have regard to the same considerations. The situation under EDMO is therefore unlikely to be different in any practical sense.)
- The amount of any compensation that is payable to a third party by virtue of a decision of the authority in respect of any interference in consequence of the final order with the rights of that person. (Such a decision would be made under s. 128 (for an FMO) or ss. 136(4) or 138(3) under an EDMO.)
- Provision as to the payment of any such compensation and, for a final EDMO, provision as to the payment of compensation to any dispossessed landlord or tenant (under Sch. 6, para. 22(5)).
- Provision as to the payment by the LHA to a relevant landlord or proprietor, from time to time, of any surplus of rent or other payments that remain after the deduction of:
  - relevant expenditure; and
  - any amounts of compensation payable as mentioned above.
- Provision as to the manner in which the authority are to pay to a relevant landlord or the relevant proprietor, on the termination of the final order, any amounts of rent or other payments that remain after the deduction of:
  - relevant expenditure; and
  - any amounts of compensation payable as mentioned above.
- Provision as to the manner in which the authority are to pay, on the termination of the final order, any outstanding balance of compensation payable to a third party (and, in the case of an EDMO, compensation to a dispossessed landlord or tenant).

The authority must keep full accounts of their income and expenditure in respect of the house (s. 119(7)(a)) or dwelling (Sch. 7, para. 13(5)(a)).

The authority must also afford to each 'relevant landlord' (in the case of an FMO) or relevant proprietor (in the case of a final EDMO), and to any other person who has an estate or interest in the house, all reasonable facilities for inspecting, taking copies of and verifying those accounts. Under s. 119(8), a relevant landlord is any person who is an immediate landlord of the house or part of it.

Part 1 of the management scheme of an FMO or the management scheme of an EDMO may also state:

- the authority's intentions as regards the use of rent or other payments to meet relevant expenditure;
- the authority's intentions as regards the payment to a relevant landlord or the relevant proprietor (where appropriate) of interest;
- that the authority does not intend to recover any shortfall arising from the previous interim or final order (as the case may be), but that instead the authority intend to use rent or other payments collected during the currency of the current final order to reimburse the authority in respect of any deficit;
- the authority's intentions as regards the recovery from a relevant landlord or the relevant proprietor, with or without interest, of any amount of relevant expenditure:
  - (in the case of an FMO) that cannot be reimbursed out of the total amount of rent or other payments;
  - (in the case of a final EDMO) that was incurred under a previous interim or final EDMO.

Enforcement of the management scheme

An important way of controlling the manner in which the authority manages the property is by applying to the RPT to force the authority to comply with the scheme (s. 120 (FMOs), Sch. 7, para. 14 (final EDMOs)).

Such an application may be made by 'an affected person'. (The heading to s. 120 (relating to FMOs) is misleading. It reads: 'Enforcement of management scheme by relevant landlord', but the list of 'affected persons' is not restricted to relevant landlords.)

Who is an affected person?

The following are affected persons:

- the immediate landlord of the house or part of it (in the case of an FMO) or the relevant proprietor (in the case of a final EDMO);
- under a final EDMO, the relevant proprietor;
- any third party to whom compensation is payable by virtue of a decision of the authority.

Under a final EDMO the following are also 'affected persons':

- any third party to whom compensation is payable by virtue of an order of the RPT; and
- a lessor, lessee, licensor or licensee under a lease or licence determined by an order of the RPT and to whom compensation is payable by virtue of an order of the RPT.

On such an application the RPT may make an order requiring the authority to manage the whole or part of the house or dwelling in accordance with the management scheme, or it may revoke the order from a date specified by the tribunal.

The power of the RPT on such an application is wide. Their order may also:

- set out the steps which the authority will take to manage the dwelling in accordance with the management scheme;
- include provision varying the final order; and
- require the payment of money to an affected person by way of damages,

where 'affected person' is as defined above.

Additional requirements for a management scheme under an FMO

The management scheme under an FMO must also contain a Part 2, which should describe in general terms how the authority intends to address the matters which caused it to make the Final Management Order. The Act gives the following as illustrative examples:

- descriptions of any steps that the authority intends to take to require persons occupying the house to comply with their obligations under any lease or licence or under the general law;
- descriptions of any repairs that are needed to the property and an explanation as to why such repairs are necessary.

Additional requirements for a management scheme under a final EDMO

In the management scheme of a final EDMO, the authority must also state:

- the amount of rent which, in the opinion of the authority, the dwelling might reasonably be expected to fetch on the open market at the time the management scheme is made; and
- where the amount of rent payable to the authority in respect of the dwelling for a period is less than the amount of rent mentioned in paragraph (c) in respect of a period of the same length, provision as to the following :
  - the deduction from the difference of relevant expenditure and any amounts of compensation payable to a third party or dispossessed landlord or tenant;
  - the payment of any remaining amount to the relevant proprietor;
  - the deduction from time to time of any remaining amount from any amount that the authority are entitled to recover from the relevant proprietor.

Furniture

A property taken over by the authority may contain what the Act describes as 'furniture', which also includes fittings and other articles (s. 126(7), Sch. 6, para. 20(7)). The vast majority of residential lettings contain some fittings such as cookers, fridges or washing machines, and thus will contain furniture, even though they would not normally be thought of as 'furnished' accommodation.

While an order is in effect, the authority will have a right to possession of furniture in the property.

Furniture in houses under an IMO, FMO or SIMO

Where on the coming into effect of a Management Order, there is furniture in the house which a person occupying the house has the right to use in consideration of periodical payments to a person who is an immediate landlord of the house or a part of it (whether the payments are included in the rent payable by the occupier or not), the authority becomes vested with a right to possession of that furniture against all persons other than the occupier which continues until the order ceases to have effect (s. 126(1)-(2)).

If the owner of the furniture makes an application in writing to the authority, they may renounce their right to possession by serving a notice in writing on the owner, giving at least two weeks' notice of when the renouncement will take effect.

Q: What happens if the furniture in a house is the subject of a hire purchase agreement?

A: It will sometimes be the case that the authority's right to possession will be exercisable against more than one person – for example if the furniture is the subject of a hire purchase agreement. In that case, any of those persons may apply to an RPT for an adjustment of their respective rights and liabilities as regards the furniture (s. 126(4)).

The RPT may make an order for such an adjustment of rights and liabilities, either unconditionally or subject to such terms and conditions, as it considers appropriate. Such an order may require payment of compensation by one of the parties to the proceedings (Who will be the persons interested in the furniture, *Procedure Regulations*, reg. 33(1)) to another.

Furniture in houses under an EDMO

On the coming into effect of an EDMO, all furniture belonging to the relevant proprietor that is in the dwelling is affected. The authority will be vested with a right to possession of that furniture while the order is in force (Sch. 6, para. 20(1)-(2)). This right is subordinate to the rights of anyone who, at the time the EDMO comes into force, has a right to possession of the dwelling.

If the authority have obtained a right to possession of furniture, but have not granted a right of possession to any other person (as they would be likely to do if they were 'letting' the property), they must give up possession of the furniture to the relevant proprietor on request (Sch. 6, para. 20(4)). Although it would be sensible for any such request to be made in writing there is no requirement for writing in the act and an oral request should be sufficient. The Act does not appear to contain any power to enforce such a request and the authority's right to possession would appear to continue until they voluntarily give up possession of the furniture to the relevant proprietor.

The authority also has a power to renounce the right to possession of furniture by serving two weeks' notice on the relevant proprietor. The authority is then required to make appropriate arrangements for storage of the furniture at its own cost.

Financial arrangements at the end of an order

At the end of an order it is unlikely that the authority's income and expenditure will have balanced precisely. There are then two possibilities: either the order is followed by a final order, the management scheme of which has provided that any loss or surplus will be carried over to the final order, or the surplus or deficit will be apportioned according to the provisions of the Act.

Surpluses after an interim order

Where, on the coming to the end of an order, there is a surplus of funds on the authority's account because they have collected more in rents and other payments than they have spent on relevant expenditure and compensation to third parties, that surplus must be paid to the relevant landlord(s) or relevant proprietor(s) in such proportions as the authority thinks appropriate (s. 129(2), Sch. 7 para. 23(2)).

In the case of an Interim Management Order this must be done 'as soon as is practicable', whereas after an interim EDMO it must be done 'as soon as possible' after the end of the order.

Deficits after an interim order

Here the situation differs between Management Orders and EDMOs. Where there has been a shortfall in funds under a Management Order, the authority may recover that shortfall from any relevant landlord or landlords in whatever proportions they consider appropriate.

At the end of an interim EDMO, the authority will not in general be able to recover any shortfall, except:

- the amount of any relevant expenditure which the relevant proprietor has agreed to pay in writing (either as a condition for the revocation of the order or otherwise);
- where the relevant proprietor is a tenant under a lease in respect of the dwelling, the amount of any outstanding service charges payable under the lease.

The authority may recover any of the shortfall from the relevant proprietor if it considers that the relevant proprietor unreasonably refused to consent to the creation of a 'lease' or 'licence' while the order was in force.

Termination of final orders

The management scheme will set out whether and in what manner sums are payable to any relevant landlord or the relevant proprietor; to any third party; and – in the case of a final EDMO – to a dispossessed landlord or tenant. Any such sums must be paid out at the end of the order as provided in the management scheme.

Under an FMO, the management scheme will govern whether any sums are payable to the authority at the end of the order.

Under a final EDMO, the authority may recover any deficit from the relevant proprietor in the same way as it would at the end of an interim EDMO.

Enforcement of deficits owed to the authority

Any sum recoverable from a relevant landlord or the relevant proprietor is, until it is recovered, a charge on the house or dwelling which gives the authority all the powers of a mortgagee under a deed, namely the powers of sale, lease, accepting surrender of leases and appointment of a receiver.

The charge is a legal charge registrable as a local land charge.

9
Overcrowding notices

The Act introduces another tool available to local authorities for the control of HMOs: the Overcrowding Notice. Overcrowding Notices may only be used for HMOs that do not need to be licensed and for which there is no Management Order currently in force.

The local authority has the right to serve an Overcrowding Notice – it does not need to seek permission of a court or tribunal, although there is a right of appeal to a Residential Property Tribunal.

The local authority may serve an Overcrowding Notice where it considers that an excessive number of persons is, *or is likely to be*, accommodated in the HMO concerned. Note our emphasis, the local authority may serve an Overcrowding Notice based on its assessment of what is likely to happen in respect of an HMO, *even if it is not overcrowded*.

The local authority may serve the notice on one or more of the following (who are known as 'relevant persons'):

- anyone having an estate or interest in the HMO concerned;
- anyone managing or having control of it.

It seems likely that managing agents will usually be among those served with an Overcrowding Notice.

Methods of enforcement

At least seven days before serving an Overcrowding Notice, the local authority must:

- inform in writing every relevant person, whether or not the authority intend to serve a notice on that person; and
- ensure that (as far as reasonably possible) every occupier of the HMO concerned is aware of the authority's intention (s. 139(3)).

This means that any mortgagee (who will have an interest in the property) must be given at least seven days' notice in writing, otherwise the subsequent Overcrowding Notice will be invalid. While notices to relevant persons must be in writing, there is no reason why a local authority should not inform occupiers of their intention orally – for example by making a visit to the property.

The local authority must give an opportunity, to any of the above people they have informed of their intention to serve a notice, of making representations about the proposal to serve an Overcrowding Notice.

The local authority may then serve the notice, which takes effect 21 days after service unless an appeal is made.

Contents of the Overcrowding Notice

The Overcrowding Notice must contain the following:

- a statement, for each room, of the maximum number of people for whom the local authority considers the room to be suitable for sleeping; or
- a statement by the local authority that it does not consider the room to be suitable as sleeping accommodation;

and either

- the requirement prescribed by s. 141 not to permit excessive numbers of persons to sleep in the house in multiple occupation; or
- the requirement prescribed by s. 142 not to admit new residents if the number of persons is excessive.

Prevention of overcrowding generally – the s. 141 requirement

The s. 141 requirement is that the person on whom the notice is served must refrain from permitting either of the following:

- a room to be occupied as sleeping accommodation 'otherwise than in accordance with the notice' – presumably this is intended to mean in accordance with the local authority's statement for each room in the property (otherwise the requirement would be circular);
- persons to occupy the HMO as sleeping accommodation in such numbers that it is not possible to avoid persons of opposite sexes who are not living together as husband and wife sleeping in the same room (s.141(1)): for the purposes of this requirement it is assumed that each room is not occupied by more than the number of persons specified in the notice, and children under the age of 10 are ignored (s. 141(2)).

In the case of a landlord or licensor, the s. 141 requirement seems only to require them not to 'permit' either state of affairs. Where the tenancy or licence agreement does not specify a maximum number of persons to be occupying rooms in terms that would satisfy s. 142, and does not give the landlord the power to exclude sufficient people to comply with s. 142, it is unclear whether the landlord is required to take any further steps (for example by serving a s. 21 notice). If a landlord has no legal right to prevent over-occupation, it would appear that they do not breach the s. 141 requirement.

Similarly a mortgagee, on whom a notice might be served, is very unlikely to have any legal power to prevent over-occupation, so would also not be in breach of s. 142.

Requirements as to new residents – the s. 142 requirement

The s. 142 requirement exactly mirrors that of s. 141. In this case the person served with the notice must prevent:

- a room from being occupied by a new resident as sleeping accommodation otherwise than in accordance with the notice; or

- a new resident from occupying any part of the HMO as sleeping accommodation if that is not possible without persons of opposite sexes who are not living together as husband and wife sleeping in the same room.

Again, in many cases a landlord may not be able to specify which room in a property a new tenant or licensee may occupy.

Consequences of disobeying the notice

Contravention of an Overcrowding Notice is a summary offence, for which the maximum fine is at level 4 on the standard scale (currently £2,500). Any person on whom the notice is served has a defence of reasonable excuse.

Appealing against an Overcrowding Notice

Any 'person aggrieved' by an Overcrowding Notice may appeal to an RPT (s. 143(1)). This means that there is no restriction on who may make an appeal. There may be people who are not relevant persons but who have a financial or other non-proprietary interest in the property that would wish to appeal the making of an order. It might also be the case that a member of an occupier's family, or a member of their community, might wish to challenge the detail of the notice.

An appeal must be made within 21 days of the date of the service of the notice (s. 143(1)).

If an appeal is brought against the service of an Overcrowding Notice, the notice does not come into operation until the RPT has made a decision and the time for bringing a further appeal to the Lands Tribunal has run out, or if an onward appeal is made to the Lands Tribunal, until a decision is given on that appeal. The withdrawal of an appeal is treated as if the appeal had been determined (s.143(5)(a)).

Q. What happens if an appeal is late?
A. An RPT may allow an appeal out of time if it is satisfied that there was good reason for not bringing the appeal in time and also good reason for any delay in asking permission to appeal out of time.

The hearing on appeal to the RPT is by way of a complete re-hearing – so the Tribunal does not have to address whether the local authority made an error in serving the notice, but has to look at the notice afresh and make a new decision. The RPT may take into account facts which were not known to the local authority at the time they made a decision to serve the notice, and the RPT may not only confirm or quash the notice, they may also vary its terms (s. 143(3)).

Revocation and variation of an Overcrowding Notice

Any 'relevant person', that is (a) any person who has an estate or interest in the HMO concerned, or (b) any other person who is a person managing or having control of it, may apply to a local authority asking it to:

- revoke the notice;
- vary the notice so as to allow more people to be accommodated in the HMO concerned.

There is no provision for an application to be made to decrease the number of permitted occupiers.

The local authority must give its decision within 35 days, though that period may be extended by the relevant person in writing.

If the local authority refuses the relevant person's request, or fails to give its decision within 35 days or such further period as the relevant person has permitted, then the relevant person may appeal to the RPT.

Such an appeal is treated in the same way as an appeal against an Overcrowding Notice, except that the tribunal may only vary the notice in a manner in which the local authority would have been able to do on the application. In particular, the tribunal may not decrease the number of permitted occupiers under the notice.

Withdrawal of notices

The authority may withdraw a notice made under s. 142 (which imposes requirements as to new residents) and replace it with a notice made under s. 141 (imposing requirements as to overcrowding generally) (s. 140(4)). There does not appear to be any other explicit power that would permit a local authority to withdraw a notice once it has been given.

Part 4

Tenancy Deposit Protection

10
Tenancy deposits

For the individual private landlord, it is probably the need to register tenants' deposits which represents the most significant effect of the *Housing Act* 2004. This requirement has certainly led to a great deal of anger among landlords, as the authors have discovered while speaking to them!

The legislation on tenancy deposit protection (TDP), comprising just four sections, is relatively limited compared to other parts of the Act. The four sections are supplemented by Sch. 10 and a couple of sets of regulations which are identical in England and Wales. Therefore one would assume that the system is relatively simple. Unfortunately the system is complicated slightly by the need to take into account the different rules of the various deposit protection schemes.

What is TDP?

Tenancy deposit protection is designed to prevent unscrupulous landlords from unfairly retaining tenant deposits at the end of their tenancies. It provides for deposits to be registered with one of three approved schemes. These schemes offer protection to the tenant, by providing adjudication services for free, making it easier for tenants to dispute unreasonable deductions.

Why bother?

The government has made no secret of its intention to introduce some form of deposit protection. As early as 1998 the government had taken note of a report by the National Association of Citizens Advice Bureaux which suggested that almost half of tenants had all or part of their deposit unreasonably withheld. As a pilot, a voluntary scheme operated by the Independent Housing Ombudsman was introduced. However, government made clear that they would legislate if the landlords did not get involved in the voluntary scheme. Few landlords or agents signed up for the scheme, and therefore the government took the decision to introduce a mandatory system, which they did as part of the *Housing Act* 2004.

What does it apply to?

TDP only applies to assured shorthold tenancies (ASTs) where a monetary deposit is being taken from the tenant. Situations where a different type of tenancy is granted, such as an assured tenancy, or where no deposit is taken, are not covered by TDP.

How does it work?

The method of operation of TDP is relatively simple. Any person taking a deposit is required to register it with one of the three approved schemes within 14 days from the deposit being taken. They must also provide the tenant with certain information in relation to the tenancy and the scheme which is protecting the deposit. At the end of the tenancy the tenant is notified of the deductions that are to be made from their deposit, and they can then either agree these or lodge a dispute, either with the deposit protection scheme that is protecting their deposit, or through the courts. The schemes are all required to provide some form of dispute resolution system, and either this or the court will decide on the appropriateness of the deductions and will then award the deposit accordingly.

Dispute resolution

Under para. 10 of Sch. 10 to the Act all TDP schemes must provide some form of dispute resolution process to allow for deposit disputes to be resolved without the need to involve the courts. However, it is not permissable to make the process mandatory. All the schemes operate a form of paper-based adjudication in order to meet this requirement.

Evasions

The fairly limited scope of TDP has led some landlords to seek ways to evade the provisions. In the main, these represent a triumph of hope over practicality. The forms of evasion basically fall into three categories:

1 Not granting an AST.
2 Not taking or appearing not to take a deposit.
3 Using some other form of security.

Some landlords have noticed that TDP applies solely to ASTs, and have sought to avoid the provisions by granting some other form of tenancy. This is only a moderately successful system. Following the case of *Antoniades v Villiers* [1988] 3 All ER 1058 the courts have been careful to prevent 'sham' agreements that seek to evade statutory protection. The courts will always look at the facts of the tenancy when trying to determine what sort of tenancy exists. Therefore some of the more constructive methods, such as getting the tenant to form a company and letting to that, are unlikely to work unless it can clearly be shown that the company was intended by both parties to be the tenant and that they all understood what was being lost by so doing (see *Kaye v Massbetter Ltd* [1991] 2 EGLR 97, CA). The courts will always look at the facts of the tenancy when trying to determine what sort of tenancy exists, rather than the form imposed on it by the landlord. It is possible for landlords to willingly grant an assured tenancy and avoid TDP this way. However, as assured tenants have security of tenure for life, this may be a case of cutting off one's nose to spite one's face!

Some landlords have simply decided not to take a deposit at all. This is a perfectly acceptable method of avoiding TDP and it does not prevent the landlord from having recourse to the courts if the tenant damages the property.

Other landlords have tried to get round the problem by taking a deposit and calling it something else. For example, some landlords have asked tenants to pay two months' rent in advance and have then refunded a month of rent at the end of the tenancy. Alternatively, landlords have charged a higher rental sum and then given the tenants back a 'discharge bonus'. Such tactics are simply ineffective. Section 213(8) of the Act defines a deposit as:

'a transfer of property intended to be held (by the landlord or otherwise) as security for—
(a)   the performance of any obligations of the tenant, or
(b)   the discharge of any liability of his, arising under or in connection with the tenancy'.

This is a very wide definition and is more than sufficient to cover all the methods of avoidance mentioned here.

There are landlords who have sought to use some alternative method of gaining security from their tenants. The taking of a deposit which 'consists of property other than money' is forbidden by s. 213(7) so the taking of other valuables as a deposit will be ineffective. Such a landlord would not be able to recover possession by serving a s. 21 notice unless and until the property taken as deposit is returned to the tenant.

Potentially, a landlord who took property as a deposit could get into even greater difficulties as, should that property be lost or destroyed it could not be returned and the landlord would then never be able to serve a s. 21 notice, as there is no other form of remedy available.

Some landlords, who are particularly concerned about the problem of tenants who fail to pay their last month's rent in order to use it to pay their deposit on their next accommodation, have sought to force tenants to pay more rent in advance, usually two months' rather than the normal one. However, this solution largely misunderstands the problem. Taking two months' rent in advance means that tenants will not have to pay rent for the last two months of the tenancy and does not prevent a tenant refusing to make the last payment.

Types of scheme

There are three approved schemes, one custodial and two insurance-based. The custodial scheme operates by taking custody of the tenancy deposit and holding it until the end of the tenancy, at which time it will disburse the monies as appropriate. The two insurance schemes allow their member landlords or agents to hold the deposit themselves, and they both hold insurance policies which guarantee that the deposit will be returned to the tenant should the landlord or agent lose or otherwise withhold the money unreasonably. Naturally the insurer will then pursue the member through the courts for the return of their money! Although all three schemes will, subject to certain requirements, accept anyone as a member, the two insurance schemes were set up to cater to certain sectors of the market and their pricing structures are set accordingly.

The providers

The three scheme providers are:

Deposit Protection Service (DPS) – www.depositprotection.co.uk
This is the custodial scheme run by Computershare on behalf of the government. It has contracted with the Chartered Institute of Arbitrators to provide its dispute resolution service.

The Dispute Service (TDS) – www.thedisputeservice.co.uk
This is an insured scheme backed by the NAEA, ARLA, and the RICS and previously operated a dispute resolution service for tenancy deposits used by some lettings agents. It has therefore continued to be primarily targeted at providing cover via lettings agents. It provides its own internal dispute resolution service.

Tenancy Deposit Solutions Ltd (TDSL) – www.mydeposits.co.uk
This is an insured scheme backed by the NLA and underwritten by Fraser Hamilton. It is primarily aimed at private landlords. The Chartered Institute of Arbitrators has contracted to provide its dispute resolution service.

Obligations in detail

The basic obligations of TDP are set out in s. 213 of the Act, most specifically in subss. (5) and (6). These require that the landlord provide information to the tenant in a prescribed form within 14 days of the date that the landlord receives the deposit.

Regulation 2 of SI 2007/797 sets out in detail the prescribed information that must be given to the tenant:

'2.—(1) The following is prescribed information for the purposes of section 213(5) of the Housing Act 2004 ('the Act')—

(a)   the name, address, telephone number, e-mail address and any fax number of the scheme administrator of the authorised tenancy deposit scheme applying to the deposit;

(b)   any information contained in a leaflet supplied by the scheme administrator to the landlord which explains the operation of the provisions contained in sections 212 to 215 of, and Schedule 10 to, the Act;

(c)   the procedures that apply under the scheme by which an amount in respect of a deposit may be paid or repaid to the tenant at the end of the shorthold tenancy ('the tenancy');

(d)   the procedures that apply under the scheme where either the landlord or the tenant is not contactable at the end of the tenancy;

(e)   the procedures that apply under the scheme where the landlord and the tenant dispute the amount to be paid or repaid to the tenant in respect of the deposit;

(f)   the facilities available under the scheme for enabling a dispute relating to the deposit to be resolved without recourse to litigation; and

(g)   the following information in connection with the tenancy in respect of which the deposit has been paid—

(i)   the amount of the deposit paid;

(ii)   the address of the property to which the tenancy relates;

(iii)   the name, address, telephone number, and any e-mail address or fax number of the landlord;

(iv)   the name, address, telephone number, and any e-mail address or fax number of the tenant, including such details that should be used by the landlord or scheme administrator for the purpose of contacting the tenant at the end of the tenancy;

(v)   the name, address, telephone number and any e-mail address or fax number of any relevant person;

(vi)   the circumstances when all or part of the deposit may be retained by the landlord, by reference to the terms of the tenancy; and

(vii)   confirmation (in the form of a certificate signed by the landlord) that—

(aa) the information he provides under this sub-paragraph is accurate to the best of his knowledge and belief; and

(bb) he has given the tenant the opportunity to sign any document containing the information provided by the landlord under this article by way of confirmation that the information is accurate to the best of his knowledge and belief.

(2) For the purposes of paragraph (1)(d), the reference to a landlord or a tenant who is not contactable includes a

landlord or tenant whose whereabouts are known, but who is failing to respond to communications in respect of the deposit.'

This is a fairly detailed and stringent set of requirements and poses a serious problem. Not all the schemes automatically provide tenants with all the necessary information to comply with reg. 2. Notably, the DPS scheme leaves it to the landlord to supply a substantial amount of this information, and most particularly the information required by reg. 2(g). This is a potential minefield for landlords who have properly registered their deposits and may believe that they are fully compliant with TDP. Many of these landlords have failed to provide appropriate prescribed information to the tenant and they will therefore find themselves in violation of the law in relation to TDP, and subject to the penalties set out below. A sample document which will fill in the gaps left by the DPS scheme and thereby satisfy the requirements of reg. 2 can be found in Appendix F.

Penalties

The penalties for not registering a deposit or complying with scheme rules are fairly severe. They are specified in s. 214 of the Act. Under this section if, at the time a tenant makes application to the Court, a landlord has not complied with the initial requirements of an approved scheme, has not provided the information prescribed by SI 2007/797, or has failed to register the deposit at all, then the court must order that the deposit is returned to the tenant or that it is paid into the custodial scheme. The court *must* also require the landlord to pay to the tenant a sum equivalent to three times the tenancy deposit. The key problem with this section from a landlord's point of view is that a landlord who had failed to register a deposit or has not complied with scheme rules and whose tenant then stops paying the rent could have real difficulties recovering possession of the property. If, as is common, a landlord were to issue proceedings for rental arrears citing ground 8 of Sch. II to the *Housing Act* 1988, the tenant could immediately defend and counter-claim on the basis that the tenancy deposit was not correctly protected. The tenant could then expect to be paid three times the deposit and would be able to use this as an equitable set-off against the rent arrears claim, thus potentially defeating the landlord's right to possession.

In addition to the financial penalties, any landlord who has not registered a deposit or who is in breach of the rules of a scheme, is unable to give a tenant a notice pursuant to s. 21 of the *Housing Act* 1988 (as amended). In short, this means that landlords who have not registered deposits will be largely unable to recover possession of their properties unless the tenant is in breach of some term of the tenancy agreement.

The penalties are relatively draconian but are designed to encourage tenants to take action against landlords who are not protecting deposits. The government thereby intends that the scheme will be policed by tenants, as they will have the incentive of gaining money from their landlords. It will also allow tenants to submit a defence to a s. 21 notice on the basis that the deposit is unprotected. However, this relies on tenants actually being aware of their rights and being prepared to exercise them.

Return of property

Section 214(5) gives the court the power to demand the return of any property that has been taken as a deposit in contravention of s. 213.

Which scheme?

It is often hard for landlords or lettings agents to decide which scheme they should join. All the schemes have their own advantages and disadvantages. The table below summarises these from the landlord/agent point of view. There is no real purpose in looking from the tenant's point of view, as the tenant has no say in what scheme is used.

Scheme	Advantages	Disadvantages
Deposit Protection Service	Free to use.	No option for landlord/agent to keep interest on tenant's deposit monies. Does not fully satisfy the requirements of SI 2007/797. Does not allow overseas landlords to join.

	Tenancy Deposit Solutions Ltd	Allows landlord/agent to retain interest on tenant's deposit monies.	Makes a charge for membership and per tenancy. Aimed primarily at landlords.	
	The Dispute Service Ltd	Allows landlord/agent to retain interest on tenant's deposit monies. Automatically satisfies all requirements of SI 2007/797 provided rules are followed. Allows for time limits on deposit return to be altered by agreement.	Makes a charge for membership. Requires the insertion of special clauses into the tenancy agreement. Aimed primarily at letting agents.	

For an individual private landlord the DPS scheme may be the most attractive as it is free. However, some landlords have chosen to use one of the two insured schemes in order to retain some measure of control over the process. For an agent the position is a little more complex as, while they can of course use the DPS scheme, many agents use the interest on tenancy deposits as a part of their income stream. Agents who are holding a small number of deposits will probably be better served by the Tenancy Deposit Solutions scheme as its charging structure is more suited to this, while agents with larger numbers of tenancies will probably find the Dispute Service scheme to be more economic as this scheme charges a flat membership fee rather than charging per tenancy. Members of ARLA or a similar body will probably prefer the Dispute Service scheme as they will qualify for a discounted membership fee.

Taking of a Deposit

The wording of the Act in regards to the taking of the deposit is a little unclear. This has led to a certain amount of confusion as to exactly at what stage the deposit needs to be protected. Section 213(1) of the Act states that a deposit 'as from the time when it is received' must be held within an authorised scheme. This leads to the conclusion that protection must occur as soon as the tenant pays the deposit monies to the landlord or his authorised agent. Indeed s. 212(9) of the Act clearly states that 'references to a landlord or landlords in relation to any shorthold tenancy or tenancies include references to a person or persons acting on his or their behalf in relation to the tenancy or tenancies'. Therefore any money paid to an agent authorised to take a deposit is the same as a payment to the landlord. This has created the slightly odd position that deposits which were taken before 6 April 2007, when TDP came into force, are not required to be protected even if they were taken with reference to a tenancy which began after 6 April. It has also caused confusion where deposits are being taken well in advance of a tenancy beginning, as is often the case with student lets for example. These deposit monies will still need to be registered within 14 days of being taken even though the tenancy to which they relate has yet to begin.

Landlord or agent?

There is some degree of uncertainty as to whether it is the responsibility of the landlord or his lettings agent to protect a tenancy deposit. This is particularly the case where the agent is only instructed to find a tenant for the property.

The CLG has issued guidance on the matter (see www.communities.gov.uk/ housing/ rentingandletting/ privaterenting/ tenancydepositprotection/ let-only) which sets out the position as they see it.

The nature of the responsibility basically comes down to the contractual arrangement between the landlord and agent. If the agreement between them is that the landlord will protect the deposit, then he will need to make arrangements to do so. If the deposit is not protected within the 14-day period from it being received by the agent then the landlord will be liable to the tenant.

Even if the agent has not yet released the deposit to the landlord then the landlord will still need to ensure that a sum equivalent to the deposit monies has been placed with one of the protection schemes.

If, however, the agreement is that the agent will protect the deposit, then the agent will hold the primary responsibility for protecting the deposit under s. 212(9). If the agent fails to protect the deposit the landlord will still be liable to the tenant but he will be able to pursue the agent for their failings.

Adjudication (what is it?)

Adjudication is a process where a dispute is resolved by an independent party – the adjudicator – without involvement of the court. It is important to realise that adjudication is not the same as arbitration and is not subject to the *Arbitration Act 1996*. In *London & Amsterdam Properties Ltd v Waterman Partnership Ltd* [1999] BLR 93 adjudication was described as follows:

> 'Adjudication gives rise to a provisional determination which is only binding until the dispute is arbitrated,

litigated or agreed. Adjudication further is subject to very restrictive time limits, and no matter how complex the dispute "one size fits all".'

While the decisions are only provisional, they are binding until such time as they are referred to arbitration or litigation or until the parties agree to alter their affects. Despite their provisional nature, adjudication decisions are enforceable by use of the courts summary judgment procedure provided by Part 24 of the *Civil Procedure Rules* (see www.justice. gov.uk/civil/procrules_fin/contents/parts/part24.htm). All the dispute resolution schemes under TDP require that parties agree to accept the results of adjudication in advance to circumvent the non-binding nature of adjudication. However, it is worth noting that, as was said in *Amsterdam Properties*, adjudication is intended to be a quick and interim solution. Therefore it is unlikely to be suitable for complex deposit disputes where the right to go to court should be exercised instead.

Questions, questions

The confused nature of tenancy deposit protection has led to a large number of questions being asked. Here we have tried to answer some of the most common ones.

Q: If I renew a tenant's lease that began before the TDP came into force, do I have to hold the deposit under a scheme?

A: This is an important question, on which the authors disagree.

One view is that a replacement tenancy is defined by s. 21(7) of the *Housing Act* 1988 (as amended) as a new tenancy which comes onto being on the coming to an end of an assured shorthold tenancy where the parties to the tenancy and property involved are the same as under the previous tenancy. Therefore any renewed tenancy will be a replacement tenancy. TDP applies to replacement tenancies that come into force after 6 April 2007, so deposits held for these tenancies will need to be protected. This view is the one adopted by the Government.

Another view is that the TDP only requires a deposit to be kept in accordance with a scheme from the day on which it is received. Where no new deposit is paid on renewal, there would be no need to hold the deposit under a scheme.

We advise that the deposit for any renewal tenancy should be held under a scheme, where possible, as a precautionary measure.

Q: What if I ask for a small additional sum for deposit? Does that mean I have to put the whole sum in the scheme?

A: No. In theory there is no need to hold anything other than the deposit which has been paid over under a scheme. As a practical matter it is almost certainly better to pay the whole deposit into the scheme, since many adjudicators would be unhappy with trying to adjudicate on only a part of a deposit. It may also create needless administrative complexity if parts of a deposit are subject to a scheme and parts are not.

Q: If a tenant sues a landlord for failing to comply with the TDP scheme, can the landlord comply before the court hearing and avoid the 3xdeposit penalty?

A: Here again, the authors are in disagreement.

A tenant might argue that s. 214(2) states that if the court is satisfied 'on application' that the requirements of TDP have not been met, then if the tenant has issued proceedings for non-compliance it is already too late for the landlord to do anything and he will not be able to avoid the penalties.

An alternative view, that is more supportive of landlords, is that the penalty is only payable if the court 'is satisfied' that the landlord has failed to comply. The use of the present tense implies that the court must assess the question of compliance at the hearing of the application. If the landlord has complied by that stage, the penalty should not be ordered (although the tenant might be entitled to their costs in the circumstances).

Q: Can a tenant raise the failure to comply at a hearing for possession without having pleaded it, and get the 3xdeposit penalty?

A: Yes. If the claim is one for rent arrears, the tenant's right to a penalty might be treated as a sum that could be set off against any existing rent arrears and thus constitute a defence.

Q: If I accept a deposit guarantee scheme (like that of Crisis Smartmove), do I have to comply with the TDP? If so, how?

A: This will depend on how the scheme works. If no money is being taken and the landlord is simply being offered a guarantee by a charity, local authority, company or some other individual or organisation, then no money is being taken and the deposit does not need to be protected. If, however, money is being given to the landlord then this will fall under TDP and the deposit will have to be protected.

Q: I am changing agent and moving the deposit but it was taken before 6 April 2007. Does it now have to be registered?

A: This is a hard question to answer. It could be said that the deposit is being taken by a new person and, as the Act does not distinguish between landlord and agent, it should now be protected. However, it could equally well be argued that the original agent had taken the deposit on behalf of the landlord and was acting as his representative. Merely passing it to a new representative of the landlord does not constitute the payment of the deposit to a new person and therefore it does not need to be registered. In such a situation it would probably be wise to register the deposit, to be safe.

Q: I took a deposit before 6 April 2007 for a tenancy that began after that date. Do I have to register it? OR I am taking a deposit now for a tenancy that does not begin for some time. When does the deposit need to be registered?

A: No. The legislation applies at the time the deposit is taken, not at the time the tenancy begins. Therefore deposits taken before 6 April 2007 do not need to be registered, even if the tenancies they relate to began after that date. Equally, the requirement to register the deposit begins from the time the deposit is taken, not the date of the tenancy starting, so there may be cases where a deposit must be registered before the start of a tenancy.

Q: Help! I took a deposit for a tenancy registered under the scheme run by the Dispute Service Ltd, but I did not include the required clauses in the tenancy agreement. Can I do anything?

A: If you have not followed the rules of a scheme, then you will be liable to the penalties set out in ss. 214 and 215 of the Act. However, there is nothing to stop you moving the deposit to a different scheme with different rules and following the rules of that scheme.

Q: As an agent, I make a habit of taking a holding deposit once tenants have expressed an interest in a property in order to ensure that our costs are covered if they withdraw from the tenancy. Does this money have to be protected?

A: No. A holding deposit (technically known as 'earnest money') is not money being taken as security for the tenant's compliance with a term of the tenancy and therefore is not covered by TDP legislation. However, if it is your habit to then put the holding deposit towards the tenancy deposit, the monies will need to be protected within 14 days of this occurring.

Q: Can I make a charge to the tenant for my costs in using a scheme?

A: Yes, so long as the charge is reasonable and is an accurate reflection of the genuine costs of protecting the deposit.

Post-tenancy procedure

The precise post-tenancy procedure depends on the scheme in which the landlord has decided to protect the deposit. The procedure for the custodial scheme is set down by legislation; the two insured schemes have greater freedom to set their own rules. The first stage will be for the landlord to notify the tenant of any deductions he proposes to make from the tenant's deposit. This must be done within ten days, unless the deposit is protected by the TDS scheme in which case the tenancy agreement will set out the time limit. If the parties are unable to come to an agreement about the deductions, or the time limit is exceeded, then a dispute will be triggered. At that point the parties will need to decide whether they wish to use the ADR system provided by the scheme or whether they wish to go to court. If ADR is to be used, then any monies held in accordance with an insured scheme which are in dispute will be required to be paid to the scheme. At that point the parties will either need to submit their evidence to a scheme adjudicator or prepare for a court case.

Disappearing tenants or landlords

One of the difficulties all schemes face is how to deal with situations where one of the parties to the dispute has disappeared or is no longer contactable. Normally this is a problem regarding tenants, but landlords can also drop out of sight unexpectedly. The custodial scheme has a clear process, set out in paras 4A, 4B and 4C of Sch. 10 to the Act. The two insured schemes cannot use the same process, and have their own methods of dealing with the problem.

The custodial scheme allows either the landlord or tenant to apply to the scheme, enclosing a statutory declaration signed before a solicitor or other suitable individual setting out:

- the date the tenancy ended;
- that there has been no agreement made between the parties;
- the address details held about the other party;
- the details that are known of the other party's whereabouts.

Additionally, the landlord's declaration will need to include the amount claimed and details of how it has been calculated. On receipt of such a declaration the custodial scheme will attempt to contact the missing party. If they receive no response then they will make an adjudication in the favour of the other party and release the deposit as appropriate.

The insured schemes, as stated above, cannot use the same system as the custodial scheme. Where the tenant is unavailable at the end of a tenancy then the insured schemes will not get involved, as they only need to adjudicate where the tenant objects to deductions being made. Clearly, if the tenant is not around then it will be hard for him to object. Naturally, no scheme can prevent either party applying to court to decide the disposition of the deposit. The court can make a decision without the input of a party.

Adjudication evidence

Many landlords fail to get the adjudication they desire because they fail to provide an adjudicator with appropriate evidence for the claim they wish to make, or because they try to make an unrealistic deduction from the tenant's deposit. While the details of how to decide on an appropriate deduction are beyond the scope of this text, the following guidelines should prove helpful.

- Bear in mind that the deposit is there to compensate for genuine losses incurred by the landlord. If the landlord has not actually suffered any loss then they have no grounds to make a deduction.
- The tenant is not required to provide a 'new for old' replacement. The landlord is not entitled to get anything better than he has lost. Therefore if a carpet is five years old then the tenant does not have to buy the landlord a new carpet. In practice, this means that a deduction will need to be made from the amount claimed to take into account the age of the item claimed for.
- It is important to have a realistic expectation of a lifespan of the item being claimed for. It will be hard to convince an adjudicator, or anyone else, that a carpet has a lifespan of more than 10–15 years, or that properties do not need to be repainted at least every six years. Therefore a tenant who destroys a 17-year-old carpet is unlikely to be liable to the landlord at all, as the carpet would have needed replacing anyway.

Thinking about how to prove the case

The following list should give an idea of what is needed to successfully prove a claim:

- Check-in/check-out inventories.
- Photographs of the stains, breaks etc.
- Receipts/invoices for work done.
- Estimates of work to be done.
- Expert evidence; for example, where it is alleged by the landlord that stains in a carpet would be impossible/impractical to remove by cleaning, a letter or report from a carpet cleaning company to this effect would assist.

Conclusion

While TDP has caused a lot of heartache to landlords and agents, it is, in truth, a relatively simple system. There are uncertainties and arguments about how it operates, which are mainly due to poor drafting, but these will only affect a tiny minority of landlords who have failed to comply properly with the schemes and are seeking to avoid penalties. For many landlords, and the majority of agents, who were already holding tenants' deposits in a separate bank account and only making reasonable deductions, then the position will be largely unchanged, save for the need to do a little more paperwork. Whether the system will achieve its objective in preventing less scrupulous landlords from withholding tenants' deposits unreasonably depends entirely on how effectively failure to protect a deposit is enforced. Given that the onus is placed on tenants, then it is a matter of making sure that they are aware of their rights and the remedies available to them.

Part 5

The Residential Property Tribunal

11

The Residential Property Tribunal

Introduction

There are very many circumstances where an individual may be aggrieved by the action of their local housing authority (for instance, if the authority refuses to grant an HMO licence), and in most cases the *Housing Act* 2004 gives a right of appeal to a Residential Property Tribunal (RPT). This is the name given to a long-established body, the Rent Assessment Committee, when it is 'sitting as' an RPT – that is, when it is dealing with one of the matters described in this book.

An RPT consists of one chair, who will usually be legally qualified, together with one or two additional members (called wing members because they sit on either side of the chair), who will usually have experience of property management or valuation.

As well as appeals against various decisions by the local housing authority, there are many other circumstances where an individual or the authority may wish to obtain a decision from the RPT. The *Housing Act* 2004 sometimes describes these as 'applications' and in other cases as 'appeals'. This chapter will use the words 'application' and 'applicant' for both situations.

For the purposes of the applications considered in this book, the rules of procedure that govern the RPT are the the *Residential Property Tribunal Procedure (England) Regulations* 2006 (SI 2006/831) and the the *Residential Property Tribunal Procedure (Wales) Regulations* 2006 (SI 2006/1641, W. 156). The two sets of rules are identical, save that the Welsh regulations are written in inclusive language (avoiding the use of the word 'he'). The fees charged by the RPT are governed by the *Residential Property Tribunal (Fees) (England) Regulations* 2006 (SI

2006/830) and the *Residential Property Tribunal (Fees) (Wales) Regulations* 2006 (SI 2006/1642 W. 157) in England and Wales respectively. There is currently no difference between the fee regimes in the two areas.

The Overriding Objective

The most important principle to understand when dealing with litigation before an RPT is the idea of the 'overriding objective' which is imposed by reg. 4. The overriding objective is for the tribunal to deal fairly and justly with any application it is considering. The tribunal must try to give effect to the overriding objective when it is exercising any of its powers under the regulations or when it interprets any regulation.

The idea of the overriding objective has been borrowed from the Civil Procedure Rules introduced in 1999 and was largely influenced by Lord Woolf, the then Master of the Rolls. The aim of including the overriding objective is to prevent an overly technical or legalistic approach to the rules and the way that the tribunal behaves. The tribunal will always keep in mind the objective of dealing justly and fairly.

Regulation 4 gives five examples of what dealing with an application fairly and justly might include:

- dealing with it in ways which are proportionate to the complexity of the issues and to the resources of the parties;
- ensuring, so far as practicable, that the parties are on an equal footing procedurally and are able to participate fully in the proceedings;
- assisting any party in the presentation of his case without advocating the course he should take;
- using the tribunal's special expertise effectively; and
- avoiding delay, so far as is compatible with proper consideration of the issues.

Getting started: how cases come before the RPT

Most cases will come before the RPT because someone has either appealed or applied to the RPT, but it is also possible for a case to be transferred from a court to the RPT.

Where there is, before a court, any question which the RPT would have jurisdiction to determine had an application been made to the RPT, the court may order the transfer of as much of the proceedings as are before it to the RPT as relate to the determination of that question.

The court may then dispose of the remaining proceedings, or it may postpone them awaiting the result of the hearing before the RPT.

> **Q: Who may make an application? Can interested parties make applications to the RPT or are there constraints?**
>
> **A:** There is no simple answer to this question. Each different form of application has different rules for who may make the application in the first place. A full list can be found in Appendix H.

Making an application

Time limits

Many applications to the RPT must be made within a specified time – 21 and 28 days being the most common – of a relevant event, for example the service of a notice. A complete table showing these time limits can be found in Appendix H. In general, no time limits are imposed on the local housing authority.

The specified time is often the date on which a decision was made by the local authority. The normal rule is that when an authority makes a decision – for example to refuse an application for an HMO licence – it must serve a notice of its decision and that notice will specify a date on which the decision was made. It is the date given in the notice that starts the time limit clock ticking, so that if the local authority are slow in serving the notice, time may be short for a prospective applicant to the RPT. Some notices depart from this general rule, so that, for example, the relevant date is the date the notice was served.

For example, prohibition orders made under the HHSRS are effective from the date the order is made and the time limit for an appeal begins on this date, but improvement notices are effective from the date that the notice is served. In LON/00AY/HIN/2006/0001 the local authority suggested that the date of service was the date the notice was posted, but the RPT took the view that the date of service was the date that the notice was received, which is almost certainly correct

It is important to note that there is also a lack of clarity as to precisely when the clock stops ticking. Does the appeal notice need to be posted prior to the end of the time limit, or does it need to be received before that date? In *R. (On the application of Lester) v London Rent Assessment Committee* [2003] HLR 53 the Court of Appeal took the view that the appeal notice had to be received prior to the expiry of the time limit. Given the origins of the RPT in the RAC, this would seem to be good law and it would therefore be wise to ensure that appeals are sent in good time and by a method that provides proof of receipt.

In most cases, the RPT has the power to dispense with the time limit, but before it does so, it must be satisfied of two things: first that there was a 'good reason' for not making the appeal or application within the time limit, and second that there was also a 'good reason' for any delay in making the application to the tribunal for the extension of time.

This emphasises the importance of making an application to the tribunal promptly even if the deadline has already been missed.

The RPT does not have a power to extend time in the following situations:

- an appeal against a refusal by the local housing authority to give approval for a particular use of premises that would otherwise be in breach of a prohibition order;
- an appeal against a temporary exemption notice under either the HMO or selective residential licensing schemes;
- an appeal against the refusal by the local housing authority to revoke an HMO declaration.

Example

In LON/00AM/HMD/2007/0002D, an appeal against the refusal the by the local housing authority to revoke an HMO declaration, the applicant had sent his appeal to the tribunal after the 28-day time limit had expired. He attempted to explain the reasons for his delay, but the tribunal refused to hear him, finding they had no jurisdiction to extend time.

An application to extend time must contain certain specified information (see below).

Contents of an application to extend time

An application to extend time must:

- be in writing;
- give reasons for the failure to make the application before the end of that period and for any further delay since then;
- include a statement that the person making the request believes that the facts stated in it are true; and
- be dated and signed.

The application

The Residential Property Tribunal Service has created a number of application forms, which may be downloaded from their website. There is no requirement in the rules that these forms should be used, though it is sensible to do so.

The regulations require all applications to contain certain common information, such as the particulars of the parties and the address of the property. For each kind of application there may also be further specified information or documents that must be supplied. A full list of these provisions is to be found in the Appendix H – they are also set out on the application forms provided by the RPTS.

For each kind of application there is a designated respondent, who must be named in the application. In many cases this will be the local housing authority. The identity of the designated respondent is given in the table attached to the application form, and also in Appendix H.

An application must also give a list of any 'interested person' who is known to the applicant. A discussion of the types of interested person is given later. There is no need to find out the name and address of any interested person if it is not known.

Example

L is the landlord of a property who has received an improvement notice requiring L to construct a rear boundary fence to the property to prevent intruders. L wants to argue that it should be his rear neighbours who construct a boundary fence (this example is taken from LON/00AM/HMD/2007/0002D).

L has 21 days from the date of service of the notice to apply to the RPT.

His application must include a copy of the improvement notice together with any material attached to it, the statement of reasons and, because he is suggesting an alternative course of action, a statement identifying that course of action with his reasons for considering it the best course. The specified respondent is, unsurprisingly, the local housing authority.

Any of the requirements as to the contents of an application may be relaxed by a tribunal – including a single member tribunal – provided that it is satisfied that the particulars and documents included with the application are sufficient to establish that the application is one that may be made to the tribunal; and that no prejudice will be caused or is likely to be caused to any party of the application.

Example

If, in the previous example, L had lost the statement of reasons, a tribunal ought to permit L to make the application without them because it is obvious what L's application is and, most importantly, the tribunal has jurisdiction to hear his application. The only other party likely to be involved in the case is the local housing authority, who already have a copy of the statement of reasons and will not be prejudiced by L's failure to supply it.

The following information must be supplied with all applications:

- the applicant's name and address;
- the name and address of the respondent where known to the applicant, or where not known, a description of the respondent's connection with the premises;
- the address of the premises;
- the applicant's connection with the premises;
- the applicant's reasons for making the application, including the remedy sought;
- where known to the applicant, the name and address of any interested person;
- a statement that the applicant believes that the facts stated in the application are true.

How to make an application

An application should be made in writing to one of the RPTS offices, depending on which region the property is located in. A list of the panel offices and their addresses is given in Appendix G. For most types of application the RPTS provides application forms, but these are not prescribed and there is no requirement to use them. There are, as yet, no provisions for making an application by fax or email or online.

Application fees

An application fee of £150 must be paid for some, but not all, types of application. A full list of applications that require a fee to be paid is to be found in Appendix H. There are only two options for paying the fee: either a postal order drawn in favour of, or a cheque payable to the Office of the Deputy Prime Minister (in England) or the National Assembly for Wales (in Wales).

The fee does not have to be paid at the same time as the application, but if it is not paid within 14 days of the application being received by the tribunal, the application is treated as withdrawn unless the tribunal is satisfied there are reasonable grounds not to do so.

Where an applicant, or their partner, is receiving, on the date of the application, one of a number of benefits, they may be entitled to have the obligation to pay fees waived. The box below shows which benefits give rise to a fee waiver. In the box the word 'couple' means:

- a man and woman who are married to each other and are members of the same household;
- a man and woman who are not married to each other but are living together as husband and wife;
- two people of the same sex who are civil partners of each other and are members of the same household; or
- two people of the same sex who are not civil partners of each other but are living together as if they were civil partners,

and for the purposes of the definition, two people of the same sex are to be regarded as living together as if they were civil partners if, but only if, they would be regarded as living together as husband and wife were they instead two people of the opposite sex.

Benefits which give rise to a waiver of fees

Anyone in receipt of the following benefits is entitled to have their fees waived by the tribunal:
- income support;
- housing benefit;
- income based jobseeker's allowance;
- working tax credit, where the gross annual income taken into account for the calculation of the working tax credit is £14, 213 or less and:
- there is a disability element or severe disability element (or both) to the tax credit received by the person or the person's partner;
- the person or the person's partner is also in receipt of child tax credit;
- guarantee credit.

Notification by the tribunal and the reply

As soon as practical after receiving the application, the tribunal must send an acknowledgement to the applicant and send a copy of the application and each document accompanying it to the respondent.

Unless the application is urgent (when no reply would normally be required from the respondent, because of the urgency of the matter), the tribunal must also send the respondent a notice specifying a date by which the respondent must send its reply to the tribunal. That date must be not less than 14 days after the date given in the notice specifying when the notice was made.

Where a notice requesting a reply has been received, the respondent must send to the tribunal within the time limit given in the notice a document called a reply.

Contents of a reply

A reply must state:

- whether or not the respondent intends to oppose the application;
- where not already included in the application, the name and address of each interested person known to the respondent; and
- the address to which documents should be sent for the purposes of the proceedings (for instance the address of a solicitor acting for the respondent).

Who is an interested person?

An interested person is someone who is not the applicant or respondent but who, for one reason or another, ought to be aware of, and have the opportunity of joining in, any application. This would include the following categories:

- Anyone who would otherwise be entitled to make the same application to the RPT.
- Where the authority intend to apply for a rent repayment order (see page 73), they must notify the person who was entitled to receive the rent or other periodical payment for occupation that they are proposing to apply for such an order, giving the person 28 days to respond. Anyone served with such a notice by the authority is an interested person in any proceedings that are commenced.
- Where someone has been served with an improvement notice, they may appeal to the RPT on the ground that one or more other persons ought to do the work or pay some or all of the costs of taking the improvement action. The appealing party must serve a copy of the notice of appeal on such a person, who is an 'interested person' in those proceedings.
- Where an authority carries out enforcement action on its own account under an improvement notice, it may appeal to an RPT on the ground that it is unlikely to recover the costs of taking the action, and that another person has profited by their actions. Such a person is an interested person in the proceedings.
- Before determining or varying a lease, a tribunal must give any sub-lessee the opportunity of being heard.
- Where a demolition order is made, the tribunal has the power, on the application of a lessor or lessee of the premises, to terminate or vary the lease. The tribunal is required to give any sub-lessee an opportunity to be heard, and such a person is an 'interested person'.
- the local housing authority (if it is not already a party).

Supply of documents to interested persons

As will be clear, many interested persons will already be aware of an application. Notwithstanding this, the RPT must send certain information to each interested person the name and address of whom it has been notified. There is no duty on the RPT to try to find the names and addresses of interested parties even if it is aware of their existence.

Information that must be sent to interested persons

- A copy of the application.
- An explanation of the procedure for applying to be joined as an applicant or respondent.
- Any other information or document which the tribunal considers appropriate.

Once the tribunal has complied with its duty to supply information to an interested person, it does not have to take any further action to keep that person informed of the proceedings – for instance by sending them further documents – unless they successfully apply to be joined in as a party.

Joining in an application

Anyone may make a request to a tribunal to be joined as a party to a existing proceedings. Such a request may be dealt with by a single tribunal member, who must decide, on the basis of the reasons given in the request, whether to grant or refuse it. The request must state whether the requesting party wishes to become an applicant or a respondent to the proceedings.

Once the tribunal has decided whether to grant or refuse the request to be joined it must send a notification of its decision to the requesting party and a a copy of its notification to all other parties. The notification must include the tribunal's reasons for coming to its decision.

Joining applications together

It is possible for a tribunal to order that two or more applications are dealt with together. There are two situations where the tribunal may do this:

1 where the applications involve related issues concerning the same premises;
2 where, although the applications involve different premises, the same parties have interests in all the premises, and similar or related issues need to be determined in all of them

> **Example**
>
> A local housing authority served four prohibition notices on four flats contained in the same building in Plymouth. The building's manager made four appeals against those notices and the tribunal decided to join the four appeals together so that they would be dealt with at the same time [CHI/00MR/HPO/2007/0001D].

Between the application and the hearing

There may be many things that happen between the application and the hearing. In particular, each party may want to obtain documents or information in the possession of the other party in order to properly prepare its case.

Information and documents

Before deciding an application (either by a hearing or in writing), the tribunal must ensure that all the other parties are supplied with a copy of any document relevant to the proceedings that the tribunal has received from any other party or from an interested person. The tribunal may supply 'sufficient extracts' of a document, though that is likely to be unusual as it would require time-consuming work by the tribunal, which in most cases is unlikely to be easier than copying. There is obviously no obligation for the tribunal to supply a document to a party that that party already has or which they have been previously supplied with.

Where a party has sent a document to the tribunal, the tribunal may order that party to send the document to any of the other parties to the application. This could be an easier option for the tribunal, but the fact that a tribunal has made such an order does not relieve them of the obligation of sending a copy to any party who has not had the document (or of course sufficient extracts from it), unless that party actually receives a copy of the document.

At a hearing, if a party has not received a relevant document (or suitable extracts from it), the tribunal must adjourn the hearing unless:

- the party consents to go ahead with the hearing;

- the tribunal considers that that person has a sufficient opportunity to deal with the matters to which the document relates without an adjournment of the hearing.

But the tribunal need only adjourn for a period which it considers will give that person a sufficient opportunity to deal with the matters to which the document relates.

Q: I attended a hearing at which I discovered that the local authority had sent to the tribunal a copy of a survey they conducted on my property. The tribunal had forgotten to send me the document with the order, so I had never seen it. The tribunal would only allow me a short 30-minute adjournment to read it. Was that right?

A: Yes. The tribunal only needs to give you sufficient time to deal with the matters raised in a document. In this case, if the points made in the survey were relatively straightforward or were not very relevant to the decision of the tribunal, 30 minutes might be enough; if, on the other hand, you would need to ask an expert of your own to comment on the report, it would be likely to be unfairly short.

Obtaining documents from another party

A tribunal may order a party to supply any other party with specified information or documents within a specified time. This process is technically known as 'discovery' in the civil courts, although it is often called 'disclosure' and both terms are often used by tribunals (strictly speaking, 'disclosure' is where you admit to having a document; 'discovery' is where you give it or a copy of it to someone else).

A tribunal may also order anyone (whether a party or not) to attend an oral hearing to give evidence, or produce documents specified in the order.

The tribunal may not order a party to produce a document that it could not be compelled to produce at a trial in a court. The two most common situations where that would apply is where the document is:

- 'without prejudice';
- privileged.

Any discussion is 'without prejudice' if it is part of a genuine negotiation to settle a dispute. Evidence of without-prejudice negotiations is not normally admitted at trials, in order to encourage parties to be candid about the difficulties of their case in negotiations without it prejudicing their trial. Learning that a party has been prepared to offer a large sum to the other might well prejudice the judge or tribunal hearing the case.

Some organisations regularly head their communications 'without prejudice', but the courts have consistently held that the label you put on a communication has little relevance. What is important is the substance. A court would ask itself, are the parties actually trying to negotiate a settlement?

In practical terms this means that a tribunal ought not to expect to see communications between the parties which are solely to do with negotiating a settlement to the claim.

Privileged communications are, roughly speaking, those made between a lawyer and their client. Again, in order to protect the right of anyone to communicate freely with their legal advisers, privileged documents are not normally admissible in court.

What if a party delays in supplying the documents or information requested?

The tribunal has the power to sanction the delaying party, for example by making an order dismissing or allowing the whole or part of an application (depending on whether the defaulting party is the applicant or respondent).

Before the hearing: interim orders

A very important power of the tribunal is to make interim orders. These have the same effect as would a final decision of the tribunal, but the effect is temporary until trial. An interim order may:

- suspend, in whole or in part, the effect of any decision, notice, order or licence which is the subject matter of proceedings before it;
- temporarily grant any remedy which it would have had power to grant in its final decision.

However, this power does not apply to an application for an Interim Management Order.

> **Example**
>
> A landlord applies for a temporary exemption notice, which is refused by the local housing authority. The landlord appeals against that decision and, at the same time, asks the tribunal to grant a temporary exemption notice as an interim measure until the hearing.
>
> A tribunal may make an interim order without giving the parties an opportunity to make any representations about it, but if it does, a party may request that the interim order be varied or set aside. Such a request may be made at a hearing, in writing or in any other means permitted by the tribunal.
>
> Once an interim order is made, it must, as soon as possible, be recorded in a document. The document must give reasons for the decision unless the order was made by the consent of all the parties.

Directions

One of the ways that a tribunal can control the litigation before it is by the giving of 'directions'. Parties involved in a case being dealt with by a tribunal can use the tribunals power to give directions in order to make the running of the case simpler for them. Careful thought given to whether to apply to a tribunal for directions can pay dividends in terms of the ability of a party to prepare its case.

What directions may a tribunal give

A tribunal may give whatever directions it considers necessary or desirable for securing the just, expeditious and economical disposal of the proceedings or any issue raised in or in connection with them. Most directions, called 'procedural directions', may be made by a single tribunal member. A few directions, which are not procedural directions, must be made by a full tribunal. The list of directions which are not procedural directions illustrates how wide are the powers of the tribunal to make directions.

Directions which must be made by a full tribunal

A direction is not a procedural direction if it:

- requires a licence to be granted under Parts 2 or 3 of the *Housing Act* 2004;
- requires any licence so granted to contain such terms as are specified in the directions;

- requires any order made under Part 4 of the *Housing Act 2004* to contain such terms as are so specified;
- directs that any building or part of a building so specified is to be treated as if an HMO declaration had been served in respect of it on such date as is so specified (without there being any right to appeal against it under s. 255(9));
- requires the payment of money by one party to the proceedings to another by way of compensation, damages or otherwise.

A party may request that the tribunal make an order. Such a request must specify the directions which are sought and the reasons for seeking them.

The tribunal also has the power to reduce or extend the time permitted for doing anything required by the regulations. It may only extend time in two circumstances:

- when it would not be reasonable to expect the person in question to comply or have complied within that time;
- when not to extend the time would result in substantial injustice.

The second option is likely to be a fairly stringent test. Failure to do something important in time simply due to lack of organisation is unlikely to be sufficient.

The tribunal may also permit the use of telephone, video link, or any other method of communication, either to make representations to the tribunal; or for the purposes of a case management conference or hearing.

In normal court procedure a witness statement ends with a statement (known as a 'statement of truth') by the author stating that they believe the facts stated in the witness statement are true. Witness statements in an RPT case do not normally require a statement of truth, but the tribunal may require a witness statement to contain one.

A tribunal may also take any other step or make any other decision which the tribunal considers 'necessary or desirable for the purpose of managing the case'.

Case management conferences

The tribunal may also order a 'case management conference', or CMC (called a 'pre-trial review' in the Act). The purpose of a CMC is to try to resolve any preliminary difficulties with the way that an application is being conducted. The tribunal may order the parties to take such steps or do such things as appear to it to be necessary or desirable for securing the just, expeditious and economical determination of the application, and it may make directions (or interim orders) as explained above.

A CMC will usually be heard by a single member tribunal, and may be postponed or adjourned if the tribunal thinks it appropriate. Although CMCs are usually less formal than a trial, any party may be represented at a CMC if they so wish. The tribunal is required to give the parties not less than seven days notice of any CMC.

Dealing with frivolous and vexatious applications

Where it appears to the tribunal that an application is frivolous or vexatious, or otherwise an abuse of process, the tribunal may dismiss the application in whole or in part. Before doing so, the tribunal must first give notice of its intention to do so to the applicant. Such a notice must specify:

- that the tribunal is minded to dismiss the application;
- the grounds on which it is minded to dismiss the application;
- the date (being not less than 21 days after the date that the notice was sent) before which the applicant may be heard by the tribunal on the question of whether the application should be dismissed.

The applicant may make a request to be heard by the tribunal before the date given in the notice. If the applicant does so, a hearing must be held and the tribunal must hear whoever attends on the question of the dismissal of the application before the application may be dismissed.

Dismissal of an application in this way is one of the grounds on which the tribunal may make a costs order against the party dismissed (see page 176).

Withdrawing

An applicant may decide that they no longer wish to continue with an application or some part of it. An applicant may only withdraw before the application is determined. The withdrawing party must notify withdrawal of the application by a signed and dated notice supplied to the tribunal:

- sufficiently identifying the application or part of the application which is withdrawn;
- stating whether any part of the application, and if so what, remains to be determined; and
- confirming that a copy of the notice of the withdrawal has been supplied to all other parties and stating the date on which this was done.

There is no need to seek permission to withdraw from an application and, in many cases, the withdrawal will take effect when the notice is supplied to the tribunal. On the other hand, there may be matters that are 'pending' which will need to be dealt with before the withdrawal takes effect.

Pending matters that delay a withdrawal

The following matters which must be dealt with before a withdrawal takes effect:

- an interim order in favour of a party has been made;
- a party has given an undertaking to the tribunal;
- payment to the withdrawing party has been ordered, whether by way of compensation, damages, costs, reimbursement of fees or otherwise;
- a party has requested an order for reimbursement of fees.

In these situations, there are two ways for the withdrawing party to bring proceedings to an end.

First, the party may send to the tribunal a written statement which has been signed by all the other parties setting out how the circumstances are to be dealt with.

Second, in situations where there is no agreement between the parties, the party may request the tribunal to give directions as to the conditions on which the withdrawal may be made. The tribunal, which may be a single member tribunal, may impose such conditions as it considers appropriate on any directions it makes. Once the tribunal has made directions, the withdrawal takes effect.

Hearings

The default position (with one exception) is that the tribunal will deal with the case without holding an oral hearing. Instead it will deal with a case simply by reading the papers and any written submissions it has been sent. The advantage of avoiding a hearing in this way are that costs need not be incurred in sending representatives or witnesses to the hearing. The disadvantage is that, if the case is a complicated one and your case is difficult, it may be better to attend to protect your interests.

Either party has a right to an oral hearing; and one will be heard if either party requests it or if the tribunal gives notice to the parties that it intends to hold an oral hearing. The latter situation will arise if the tribunal (usually a single member tribunal) decides after looking at the case file, that an oral hearing is appropriate.

Urgent oral hearings

The exception to this rule occurs when a local authority applies for an IMO as a matter of urgency. If it appears to the tribunal that certain exceptional circumstances exist, it will hold an urgent oral hearing.

Exceptional circumstances that justify an urgent oral hearing are:

1   that there is an immediate threat to the health and safety of the occupiers of the house or to persons occupying or having an estate or interest in any premises in the vicinity of the house; and
2   that, by making the interim management order as soon as possible (together where applicable with such other measures as the LHA intends to take), the LHA will be able to take immediate appropriate steps to arrest or significantly reduce the threat.

The tribunal must then notify the parties and each interested person whose name and address has been notified to it of the date of hearing, which must be not less than four days after the date that the notification was sent. Note the four days is after the date of sending, not receiving, which might give a very short time in which to prepare for an urgent oral hearing.

At the hearing, the tribunal must consider whether the exceptional circumstances do exist. If they do, it must then determine the application. If they do not the hearing must be adjourned and the tribunal will give directions. The application will then continue as normal.

Notice of hearings

Except when an urgent oral hearing has been ordered, the tribunal will normally give 21 days' notice of the time, date and place of the hearing.

Adjournments

The tribunal is completely free to postpone an oral hearing to a later date, although it must give the parties reasonable notice of the time and place at which the postponed hearing will take place. The only exception to this freedom comes when it is one of the parties that has requested a postponement.

In that case, the tribunal may only postpone the hearing if it considers it reasonable to do so. In considering making a postponement at the request of one of the parties, the tribunal must consider the grounds for the request, the time at which the request is made and the convenience of the parties.

What happens if a party fails to attend?

If one of the parties fails to appear, the tribunal may proceed with the hearing, provided it is satisfied that:

- notice had been given by the tribunal in accordance with the regulations;
- it is not satisfied that there is a good reason for the failure to appear.

Unlike the situation in a court of law, if a party fails to attend for good reason, but the case is heard in their absence, there is no power for the tribunal to re-hear the case. The dissatisfied party would have to appeal to the Lands Tribunal.

Conduct of the hearing

Some regions, in particular London, have specialised hearing centres, but tribunals may meet anywhere and may do so in buildings hired temporarily for the purpose, such as public halls.

The tribunal has complete discretion to decide the way in which the hearing is conducted – in particular the order and manner in which the parties give evidence. It is in the nature of RPT hearings that, frequently, the issues between the parties do not depend on oral evidence of fact. It is not uncommon for parties to be told at a hearing that the tribunal has read all their written evidence and representations and that either there is no need for anyone to speak, or that the tribunal will only need to hear the oral representations of the parties.

There is no restriction of the kind of evidence that may be given at a tribunal, even if the evidence would normally be inadmissible in a court of law. Furthermore, the tribunal must not refuse to admit any evidence that was presented in time, which would be admissible at law, is relevant and necessary and has not been improperly obtained.

New evidence – such as evidence not previously available, or not previously adduced, may be admitted if the tribunal consider it just and reasonable to do so. In the same way, where a party relies on a new reason which has not previously been argued, the tribunal may permit them to do so, if the tribunal considers it just and reasonable to do so.

The reason for this flexibility appears to be that many orders of the tribunal have importance beyond the parties and are made in the public interest. For example, an interim management order might be made for the protection of occupiers of an unlicensed HMO. A failure by the local housing authority to properly prepare their case, should not prevent the tribunal making the order if it considers that it should.

Nevertheless, a change in a party's case will have negative consequences for the other party to compensate this the tribunal may use its very limited costs powers to compensate the affected party. For example, in LON/00AG/ HMT/2006/0003D, the council had refused to grant a temporary exemption notice on the ground that modifications proposed by the applicant, which would have required listed building consent, would have been refused. By the date of the hearing the council had withdrawn this argument but chose to run a different one. Despite having succeeded, the council were ordered to pay £500 in costs to the applicant by the tribunal.

Each party has the right to give relevant evidence, call witnesses, question any witness, and address the tribunal on the evidence and law and generally on the subject matter of the application. The wording of the regulations would appear to permit the tribunal to restrict the evidence that a party gives to the relevant evidence, but not to permit the tribunal to limit cross-examination.

Assistance at the hearing

The regulations permit a party to nominate a representative who will be sent all communications by the tribunal. It appears to be assumed that a party may be represented by anyone of their choice, although this is never expressly said in the regulations.

A party who is unable to understand English is entitled to have an interpreter free of charge. Anyone requiring such assistance must apply, at the earliest possible opportunity, to the tribunal.

Hearings in private

The normal rule is that a hearing is held in public. A hearing will be held in private if the tribunal is satisfied that in the circumstances of the case and subject to the overriding objective the hearing should be held in private. The tribunal's power is a flexible one: it may order that only a part of the hearing is held in private, and it may order that information about the proceedings before the tribunal; the names and identifying characteristics of persons concerned in the proceedings; or specified evidence given in the proceedings is to be withheld from the public.

Inspections

The tribunal has a wide and flexible power to carry out inspections. The tribunal may inspect any of the premises that are the subject of an application, but they may also inspect any other premises which might assist them in determining the application and also the locality of the premises.

Where an oral hearing is to be held, it is usual for the tribunal to carry out the inspection before the oral hearing. This permits those attending to make representations based on what has been seen in the inspection. The tribunal's task is made much easier if it has made the inspection before any discussion is held.

However, this is not an absolute rule. The inspection may be held before, during or after the hearing. If it is held afterwards, there is obviously a problem that matters might arise on the inspection that have not been dealt with in the oral hearing, so the tribunal has a power to re-open the hearing, although it must give reasonable notice of the date, time and place of the reopened hearing to the parties.

Q: Can the tribunal carry out an inspection even if there is no oral hearing?
A: Yes. Whether or not the tribunal carries out an inspection is quite separate from whether there is an oral hearing. For an example, see BIR/17UB/HPO/2006/0002.

Q: Can I refuse the other party entry to my property?
A: Yes, the tribunal's jurisdiction does not give anyone any additional right to enter property that they did not already have. However, if you refuse another party entry to the property, the tribunal may refuse to carry out an inspection, as to do so might be unfair to the excluded party.

Expert evidence

The tribunal will normally have a member who is experienced in the valuation of land, which means that there will be far less need for expert evidence than there would be in front of – for example – a county court. It may still be necessary to call expert evidence. In those circumstances the party who wishes to use the expert evidence must:

- provide the tribunal with a written summary of the evidence; and
- supply a copy of that written summary to each other party at least seven days before—
  - the date of the relevant oral hearing notified in relation to the application under reg. 25; or
  - the date notified under reg. 18 upon which the application will be determined without an oral hearing.

Contents of an expert's written summary of evidence

An expert's written summary of evidence must:

- be addressed to the tribunal;
- include details of the expert's qualifications;
- contain a statement that the expert understands and has complied with his duty to assist the tribunal on the matters within his expertise, overriding any obligation to the person from whom the expert has received instructions or by whom he is employed or paid.

The rules for the form of an expert report are important. Failure to include the required details may invalidate the report and mean that the party instructing the expert will not be able to rely on it in tribunal.

Example

An expert's report had been submitted with a number of defects: it referred to another report which was not submitted and it failed to state the expert's overriding duty to the court. The RPT refused to admit the expert's evidence. The failure to include a statement of the expert's overriding duty to the court was seen as particularly serious. [LON/00AL/HPO/2006/0001].

A tribunal may make an order that a party will not be permitted to adduce expert evidence without its permission. Such an order might be made where a relatively straightforward application is before the tribunal and it does not believe that expert evidence will be necessary. If it does give permission it may specify, as a condition of that permission, that the expert's evidence is limited to particular matters; the expert must attend to give oral evidence; or the parties must jointly instruct an expert.

The decision

At the end of an oral hearing, the tribunal may wish to retire to deliberate on the decision they make. They may, but need not, choose to give their decision orally at the end of the proceedings. Whether or not the decision was given orally, once it is made it must, as soon as practicable, be recorded in a document.

The tribunal must also give its reasons for the decision it makes. The reasons must be recorded in a document as soon as practicable after the decision has been given.

A copy of both the decision document and the reasons must be sent to the parties.

A decision, once recorded, may still be corrected if there are clerical mistakes or any errors arising in it from an accidental slip or omission contained in it. This rule – known in the context of court proceedings as the 'slip rule' – is a very limited one. It applies to mistakes, such as the misspelling of a party's name, or an incorrect calculation, but not to errors of fact or law, which may only be dealt with by an appeal.

A correction must be certified either by the chair of the tribunal that made the decision or, in their absence, by another member of the tribunal. A copy of the certified correction must be sent to each of the parties.

Costs

Unlike a court, the tribunal has very limited powers to award one party's legal costs to the other. There are two main differences. First, a tribunal may only award costs in a restricted set of circumstances, and second, it may award a maximum of £500.

A tribunal may only make a costs order against a party if it has given that party an opportunity to make representations to it.

The tribunal may also order that any party reimburse the whole or part of any fee paid by another party to the application, except that a party who would not have to pay a fee because they are in receipt of benefits (as explained above in the fees section) may not be required to reimburse another party's fees.

The tribunal's power to dismiss frivolous applications will hopefully act as a protection against a party in receipt of benefit from making numerous fruitless applications.

It appears from cases decided thus far, that the tribunal is very reluctant to award any costs except in the most exceptional of cases where one party has significantly failed to act in a reasonable manner.

Grounds for the making of a costs order

- The party has failed to comply with an order made by the tribunal.
- In accordance with regulations made by virtue of para. 5(4), the tribunal dismisses, or allows, the whole or part of an application or appeal by reason of his failure to comply with a requirement imposed by regulations made by virtue of para. 5.
- In accordance with regulations made by virtue of para. 9, the tribunal dismisses the whole or part of an application or appeal made by that party to the tribunal.
- The party has, in the opinion of the tribunal, acted frivolously, vexatiously, abusively, disruptively or otherwise unreasonably in connection with the proceedings.

Onward appeals

If a party is unhappy with the decision of the RPT, it may seek permission to appeal to the Lands Tribunal. Either the RPT or the Lands Tribunal may give permission. A request to the RPT may be made orally at a hearing where the decision that is to be appealed has been made, or subsequently to the office of the tribunal in writing.

A request to the Lands Tribunal for permission to appeal should be made on Form HA1, while the actual appeal should be made on Form HA2, both available from the Lands Tribunal website (http://www.landstribunal.gov.uk). Onwards appeals from the Lands Tribunal are made to the Court of Appeal.

Permission to appeal must be sought within 21 days of the date specified in the decision. Should both the RPT and the Lands Tribunal refuse to grant permission to appeal, then the only recourse is by way of judicial review in the High Court. Such an application could only proceed on the basis that the refusal was procedurally incorrect or wrong in law and was also of exceptional importance. In the case of *R. (On the application of Sinclair Investments (Kensington) Ltd) v The Lands Tribunal* [2005] EWCA Civ 1305 the Court of Appeal held that merely being wrong in law was insufficient grounds for the granting of judicial review and that it would also be necessary to demonstrate that the error was 'sufficiently grave to justify the case being treated as exceptional'.

Miscellaneous: rules on notices and time

Where the rules require a document or notice to be supplied to any person – whether by the tribunal, a party or anyone else, the document or notice is treated as being duly supplied:

- if it is sent to the person's proper address by first class post or by special delivery, or by recorded delivery;
- if it is delivered by any other means to the person's proper address (for example by physically putting it through the letterbox);
- if, with the receiving person's written consent, it is sent to that person—
    - by fax, email or other electronic communication which produces a text received in legible form;
    - by a private document delivery service.

Where a person is legally represented, they are deemed to have given written consent if they give their fax number, email address (or equivalent) or private document delivery address on the legal representative's notepaper.

A person's proper address for these purposes is:

- in the case of the tribunal, the address of the office of the tribunal (see Appendix G);
- in the case of an incorporated company or other body registered in the United Kingdom, the address of the registered or principal office of the company or body;
- in the case of any other person the usual or last known address of that person.

In certain circumstances, the tribunal may dispense with service of a notice or document.

Circumstances where service may be dispensed with

Service may be dispensed with if the intended recipient:

- cannot be found after all diligent enquiries have been made;
- has died and has no personal representative;
- is out of the United Kingdom;

or if for any other reason a notice or other document cannot readily be supplied in accordance with the regulations.

The tribunal may either dispense with supplying the notice or document or give directions for substituted service in such other form (whether by advertisement in a newspaper or otherwise) or manner as the tribunal thinks fit.

Where it is required under the Act or the regulations that a party must provide evidence that that party has supplied any person with a document, that party may satisfy the requirement by providing a signed certificate confirming that the document was served in accordance with the requirements of this regulation.

Q: Is there a particular form of certificate I should use, or can I simply make one up?

A: The regulations do not require any particular form of certificate. All it needs to do (as well as being signed) is to say when and how the document was served.

Time

Where the time specified by the regulations for doing any act expires on a Saturday or Sunday or public holiday, it is treated as expiring on the next following day which is not a Saturday or Sunday or public holiday.

Signatures

A signature on a document may be written or produced by computer or other mechanical means, but in either case the name of the signatory must appear below the signature so that the signatory may be identified.

Appendices

Appendix A

* Amendments from SI 2007/1903 the *Licensing and Management of Houses in Multiple Occupation (Additional Provisions) (England) Regulations* 2007 are shown in italics.

Content of applications under ss. 63 and 87 of the Housing Act 2004

1. The form of statement mentioned in regulation 7(1) is:

'You must let certain persons know in writing that you have made this application or give them a copy of it. The persons who need to know about it are—

any mortgagee of the property to be licensed

any owner of the property to which the application relates (if that is not you) i.e. the freeholder and any head lessors who are known to you

any other person who is a tenant or long leaseholder of the property or any part of it (including any flat) who is known to you other than a statutory tenant or other tenant whose lease or tenancy is for less than three years (including a periodic tenancy)

the proposed licence holder (if that is not you)

the proposed managing agent (if any) (if that is not you)

any person who has agreed that he will be bound by any conditions in a licence if it is granted.

You must tell each of these persons—

your name, address telephone number and e-mail address or fax number (if any) the name, address, telephone number and e-mail address or fax number (if any) of the proposed licence holder (if it will not be you)

whether this is an application for an HMO licence under Part 2 or for a house licence under Part 3 of the Housing Act 2004

the address of the property to which the application relates

the name and address of the local housing authority to which the application will be made

the date the application will be submitted.'

2. —(1) The information mentioned in regulation 7(2)(a) is—
(a) the name, address, telephone number and e-mail address of—
   (i) the applicant;
   (ii) the proposed licence holder;
   (iii) the person managing the HMO or house;
   (iv) the person having control of the HMO or house; and
   (v) any person who has agreed to be bound by a condition contained in the licence;
(b) the address of the HMO or house for which the application is being made;
(c) the approximate age of the original construction of the HMO or house (using the categories before 1919, 1919–45, 1945–64, 1965–80 and after 1980);
(d) he type of HMO or house for which the application is being made, by reference to one of the following categories—
   (i) house in single occupation;
   (ii) house in multiple occupation;
   (iii) flat in single occupation;
   (iv) flat in multiple occupation;
   (v) a house converted into and comprising only of self contained flats;
   (vi) a purpose built block of flats; or
   (vii) other;
(e) details of other HMOs or houses that are licensed under Part 2 or 3 of the Act in respect of which the proposed licence holder is the licence holder, whether in the area of the local housing authority to which the application is made or in the area of any other local housing authority;

(f) the following information about the HMO or house for which the application is being made, *except in respect of an application in respect of a section 257 HMO—*

    (i) the number of storeys comprising the HMO or house and the levels on which those storeys are situated;

    (ii) the number of separate letting units;

    (iii) the number of habitable rooms (excluding kitchens);

    (iv) the number of bathrooms and shower rooms;

    (v) the number of toilets and wash basins;

    (vi) the number of kitchens;

    (vii) the number of sinks;

    (viii) the number of households occupying the HMO or house;

    (ix) the number of people occupying the HMO or house;

    (x) details of fire precautions equipment, including the number and location of smoke alarms;

    (xi) details of fire escape routes and other fire safety information provided to occupiers;

    (xii) a declaration that the furniture in the HMO or house that is provided under the terms of any tenancy or licence meets any safety requirements contained in any enactment; and

    (xiii) a declaration that any gas appliances in the HMO or house meet any safety requirements contained in any enactment.

(g) *where the application is being made in respect of a section 257 HMO, the following information—*

    (i) *the number of storeys comprising the HMO and the levels on which those storeys are situated;*

    (ii) *the number of self-contained-flats and, of those, the number —*

    (aa) that the applicant believes to be subject to a lease of over 21 years; and

    (bb) over which he cannot reasonably be able to exercise control;

    (iii) *in relation to each self-contained flat that is not owner-occupied and which is under the control of or being managed by the proposed licence holder, and in relation to the common parts of the HMO—*

    (aa) details of fire precautions equipment, including the number and location of smoke alarms;

    (bb) details of fire escape routes and other fire safety information provided to occupiers; and

(cc) a declaration that the furniture in the HMO or house that is provided under the terms of any tenancy or licence meets any safety requirements contained in any enactment; and

(iv) *a declaration that any gas appliances in any parts of the HMO over which the proposed licence holder can reasonably be expected to exercise control meet any safety requirements contained in any enactment.*

3. The information mentioned in regulation 7(2)(b) is—

(a) details of any unspent convictions that may be relevant to the proposed licence holder's fitness to hold a licence, or the proposed manager's fitness to manage the HMO or house, and, in particular any such conviction in respect of any offence involving fraud or other dishonesty, or violence or drugs or any offence listed in Schedule 3 to the Sexual Offences Act 2003;

(b) details of any finding by a court or tribunal against the proposed licence holder or manager that he has practised unlawful discrimination on grounds of sex, colour, race, ethnic or national origin or disability in, or in connection with, the carrying on of any business;

(c) details of any contravention on the part of the proposed licence holder or manager of any provision of any enactment relating to housing, public health, environmental health or landlord and tenant law which led to civil or criminal proceedings resulting in a judgement being made against him.

(d) information about any HMO or house the proposed licence holder or manager owns or manages or has owned or managed which has been the subject of—

    (i) a control order under section 379 of the Housing Act 1985 in the five years preceding the date of the application; or

    (ii) any appropriate enforcement action described in section 5(2) of the Act.

(e) information about any HMO or house the proposed licence holder or manager owns or manages or has owned or managed for which a local housing authority has refused to grant a licence under Part 2 or 3 of the Act, or has revoked a licence in consequence of the licence holder breaching the conditions of his licence; and

(f) information about any HMO or house the proposed licence holder or manager owns or manages or has owned or managed that has been the subject of an interim or final management order under the Act.

4. The form of declaration mentioned in regulation 7(3)(a) is as follows—

> I/we declare that the information contained in this application is correct to the best of my/our knowledge. I/We understand that I/we commit an offence if I/we supply any information to a local housing authority in connection with any of their functions under any of Parts 1 to 4 of the Housing Act 2004 that is false or misleading and which I/we know is false or misleading or am/are are reckless as to whether it is false or misleading.
>
> Signed (all applicants)
>
> Dated
>
> I/We declare that I/We have served a notice of this application on the following persons who are the only persons known to me/us that are required to be informed that I/we have made this application:

Name	Address	Description of the person's interest in the property or the application	Date of service

Appendix B

Schedule 3 of SI 2006/373 the Licensing and
Management of Houses in Multiple Occupation and
Other Houses (Miscellaneous Provisions) (England)
Regulations 2006*

* Amendments from SI 2007/1903 the *Licensing and
Management of Houses in Multiple Occupation (Additional
Provisions) (England) Regulations* 2007 are shown in italics.

Prescribed standards for deciding the suitability for occupation of an HMO by a particular maximum number of households or persons

Heating

1. Each unit of living accommodation in an HMO must be
equipped with adequate means of space heating.

Washing facilities

2. —*(1) Where all or some of the units of living accommodation
in an HMO do not contain bathing and toilet facilities for the
exclusive use of each individual household—*
(a) *there must be an adequate number of bathrooms, toilets
and wash-hand basins suitable for personal washing) for
the number of persons sharing those facilities; and*
(b) *where reasonably practicable there must be a wash hand
basin with appropriate splash back in each unit other than
a unit in which a sink has been provided as mentioned in
paragraph 4(1),*

*having regard to the age and character of the HMO, the size and
layout of each flat and its existing provision for wash-hand
basins, toilets and bathrooms.*

(3) All baths, showers and wash hand basins in an HMO must
be equipped with taps providing an adequate supply of cold and
constant hot water.

(4) All bathrooms in an HMO must be suitably and adequately
heated and ventilated.

(5) All bathrooms and toilets in an HMO must be of an adequate size and layout.

(6) All baths, toilets and wash hand basins in an HMO must be fit for the purpose.

(7) All bathrooms and toilets in an HMO must be suitably located in or in relation to the living accommodation in the HMO.

Kitchens

3. Where all or some of the units of accommodation within the HMO do not contain any facilities for the cooking of food—

(a) there must be a kitchen, suitably located in relation to the living accommodation, and of such layout and size and equipped with such facilities so as to adequately enable those sharing the facilities to store, prepare and cook food;

(b) the kitchen must be equipped with the following equipment, which must be fit for the purpose and supplied in a sufficient quantity for the number of those sharing the facilities—

(i) sinks with draining boards;

(ii) an adequate supply of cold and constant hot water to each sink supplied;

(iii) installations or equipment for the cooking of food;

(iv) electrical sockets;

(v) worktops for the preparation of food;

(vi) cupboards for the storage of food or kitchen and cooking utensils;

(vii) refrigerators with an adequate freezer compartment (or, where the freezer compartment is not adequate, adequate separate freezers);

(viii) appropriate refuse disposal facilities; and

(ix) appropriate extractor fans, fire blankets and fire doors.

Units of living accommodation without shared basic amenities

4. — (1) Where a unit of living accommodation contains kitchen facilities for the exclusive use of the individual household, and there are no other kitchen facilities available for that household, that unit must be provided with—

(a) adequate appliances and equipment for the cooking of food;

(b) a sink with an adequate supply of cold and constant hot water;

(c) a work top for the preparation of food;

(d) sufficient electrical sockets;

(e) a cupboard for the storage of kitchen utensils and crockery; and

(f) a refrigerator.

(1A) The standards referred to in paragraphs (a) and (f) of sub-paragraph (1) shall not apply in relation to a unit of accommodation where—

(a) *the landlord is not contractually bound to provide such appliances or equipment;*

(b) *the occupier of the unit of accommodation is entitled to remove such appliances or equipment from the HMO; or*

(c) *the appliances or equipment are otherwise outside the control of the landlord.*

(2) Where there are no adequate shared washing facilities provided for a unit of living accommodation as mentioned in paragraph 2, an enclosed and adequately laid out and ventilated room with a toilet and bath or fixed shower supplying adequate cold and constant hot water must be provided for the exclusive use of the occupiers of that unit either—

(a) within the living accommodation; or

(b) within reasonable proximity to the living accommodation.

Fire precautionary facilities

5. Appropriate fire precaution facilities and equipment must be provided of such type, number and location as is considered necessary.

Appendix C

Housing Act 2004 ss 61–67*

* Amendments made by SI 2007/1904 the Houses in Multiple Occupation (Certain Converted Blocks of Flats)(Modifications to the Housing Act 2004 and Transitional Provisions for section 257 HMOs)(England) Regulations 2007 and SI 2007/3231 the Houses in Multiple Occupation (Certain Blocks of Flats) (Modifications to the Housing Act 2004 and Transitional Provisions for section 257 HMOs) (Wales) Regulations 2007 (W.283)are shown in italics.

61 Requirement for HMOs to be licensed

(1) Every HMO to which this Part applies must be licensed under this Part unless—
(a)　a temporary exemption notice is in force in relation to it under section 62, or
(b)　an interim or final management order is in force in relation to it under Chapter 1 of Part 4.

(2) A licence under this Part is a licence authorising occupation of the house concerned by not more than a maximum number of households or persons specified in the licence.

(3) Sections 63 to 67 deal with applications for licences, the granting or refusal of licences and the imposition of licence conditions.

(4) The local housing authority must take all reasonable steps to secure that applications for licences are made to them in respect of HMOs in their area which are required to be licensed under this Part but are not.

(5) The appropriate national authority may by regulations provide for—
(a)　any provision of this Part, or
(b)　section 263 (in its operation for the purposes of any such provision),

to have effect in relation to a section 257 HMO with such modifications as are prescribed by the regulations.

A 'section 257 HMO' is an HMO which is a converted block of flats to which section 257 applies.

(6) In this Part (unless the context otherwise requires)—
(a) references to a licence are to a licence under this Part,
(b) references to a licence holder are to be read accordingly, and
(c) references to an HMO being (or not being) licensed under this Part are to its being (or not being) an HMO in respect of which a licence is in force under this Part.

(7) In this Part the 'person having control' in respect of a section 257 HMO is—
(a) *in relation to an HMO in respect of which no person has been granted a long lease of a flat within the HMO, the person who receives the rack rent for the HMO, whether on his own account or as an agent or trustee of another person;*
(b) *in relation to an HMO in respect of which a person has been granted a long lease of a flat within the HMO, the person who falls within the first paragraph of subsection (8) to apply, taking paragraph (a) of that subsection first, paragraph (b) next, and so on.*

(8) A person falls within this subsection if the person—
(a) *has acquired the right to manage the HMO under Part 2 of the Commonhold and Leasehold Reform Act 2002(3);*
(b) *has been appointed by the Leasehold Valuation Tribunal under section 24 of the Landlord and Tenant Act 1987(4);*
(c) *is the person who is the lessee of the whole of the HMO under a lease between him and a head lessor or the freeholder, or is the freeholder of the HMO; or*
(d) *has been appointed to manage the HMO by the freeholder, by a head lessor of the whole of the HMO, or by a person who has acquired the right to manage the HMO under Part 2 of the Commonhold and leasehold Reform Act 2002.*

(9) In this section 'long lease' means a lease that—
(a) *is granted for a term certain exceeding 21 years, whether or not it is (or may become terminable) before the end of that term; or*
(b) *is for a term fixed by law under a grant with a covenant or obligation for perpetual renewal, other than a lease by sub-demise from one which is not a long lease,*

and neither the lease nor any superior lease contains a provision enabling the lessor or superior lessor to terminate the tenancy, other than by forfeiture, before the end of that term.

62 Temporary exemption from licensing requirement

(1) This section applies where a person having control of or managing an HMO which is required to be licensed under this Part (see section 61(1)) but is not so licensed, notifies the local housing authority of his intention to take particular steps with a view to securing that the house is no longer required to be licensed.

(2) The authority may, if they think fit, serve on that person a notice under this section ('a temporary exemption notice') in respect of the house.

(3) If a temporary exemption notice is served under this section, the house is (in accordance with sections 61(1) and 85(1)) not required to be licensed either under this Part or under Part 3 during the period for which the notice is in force.

(4) A temporary exemption notice under this section is in force—
(a) for the period of 3 months beginning with the date on which it is served, or
(b) (in the case of a notice served by virtue of subsection (5)) for the period of 3 months after the date when the first notice ceases to be in force.

(5) If the authority—
(a) receive a further notification under subsection (1), and
(b) consider that there are exceptional circumstances that justify the service of a second temporary exemption notice in respect of the house that would take effect from the end of the period of 3 months applying to the first notice,

the authority may serve a second such notice on the person having control of or managing the house (but no further notice may be served by virtue of this subsection).

(6) If the authority decide not to serve a temporary exemption notice in response to a notification under subsection (1), they must without delay serve on the person concerned a notice informing him of—
(a) the decision,

(b) the reasons for it and the date on which it was made,
(c) the right to appeal against the decision under subsection (7), and
(d) the period within which an appeal may be made under that subsection.

(7) The person concerned may appeal to a residential property tribunal against the decision within the period of 28 days beginning with the date specified under subsection (6) as the date on which it was made.

(8) Such an appeal—
(a) is to be by way of a re-hearing, but
(b) may be determined having regard to matters of which the authority were unaware.

(9) The tribunal—
(a) may confirm or reverse the decision of the authority, and
(b) if it reverses the decision, must direct the authority to serve a temporary exemption notice that comes into force on such date as the tribunal directs.

Grant or refusal of licences

63 Applications for licences

(1) An application for a licence must be made to the local housing authority.

(2) The application must be made in accordance with such requirements as the authority may specify.

(3) The authority may, in particular, require the application to be accompanied by a fee fixed by the authority.

(4) The power of the authority to specify requirements under this section is subject to any regulations made under subsection (5).

(5) The appropriate national authority may by regulations make provision about the making of applications under this section.

(6) Such regulations may, in particular—
(a) specify the manner and form in which applications are to be made;

(b)   require the applicant to give copies of the application, or information about it, to particular persons;

(c)   specify the information which is to be supplied in connection with applications;

(d)   specify the maximum fees which are to be charged (whether by specifying amounts or methods for calculating amounts);

(e)   specify cases in which no fees are to be charged or fees are to be refunded.

(7) When fixing fees under this section, the local housing authority may (subject to any regulations made under subsection (5)) take into account—

(a)   all costs incurred by the authority in carrying out their functions under this Part, and

(b)   all costs incurred by them in carrying out their functions under Chapter 1 of Part 4 in relation to HMOs (so far as they are not recoverable under or by virtue of any provision of that Chapter).

64 Grant or refusal of licence

(1) Where an application in respect of an HMO is made to the local housing authority under section 63, the authority must either—

(a)   grant a licence in accordance with subsection (2), or

(b)   refuse to grant a licence.

(2) If the authority are satisfied as to the matters mentioned in subsection (3), they may grant a licence either—

(a)   to the applicant, or

(b)   to some other person, if both he and the applicant agree.

(3) The matters are—

(a)   ...

(b)   that the proposed licence holder—

    (i)   is a fit and proper person to be the licence holder, and

    (ii)   is, out of all the persons reasonably available to be the licence holder in respect of the house, the most appropriate person to be the licence holder;

(c)   that the proposed manager of the house is either—

    (i)   the person having control of the house, or

    (ii)   a person who is an agent or employee of the person having control of the house;

(d)   that the proposed manager of the house is a fit and proper person to be the manager of the house; and

(e) that the proposed management arrangements for the house are otherwise satisfactory.

(4) When deciding whether the proposed licence holder is a fit and proper person to be the licence holder the local housing authority must take into consideration whether that person has control of the HMO and the extent to which he has control over it.

(5) Sections 65 and 66 apply for the purposes of this section.

65 Tests as to suitability for multiple occupation

(1) The local housing authority cannot be satisfied that the house is reasonably suitable for occupation as a section 257 HMO if they consider that—
(a) *the common parts of the HMO; or*
(b) *any flat within the HMO other than a flat let on a long lease,*

fail to meet prescribed standards.

(1A) Where a house becomes a section 257 HMO as a result of conversion works carried out on the house after 1ˢᵗ October 2007, any flat within the HMO in respect of which a long lease is granted after that date shall be treated for the purpose of subsection (1) as though no such lease has been granted unless—
(a) *the local housing authority are satisfied that the appropriate building standards have been met in relation to that flat; or*
(b) *the local housing authority are satisfied that the lease has been granted by a person other than the freeholder or head lessor of the whole of the HMO.*

(2) ...

(3) In this section 'prescribed standards' means standards prescribed by regulations made by the appropriate national authority.

(4) The standards that may be so prescribed include—
(a) standards as to the ..., type and quality of—
    (i) bathrooms, toilets, washbasins and showers,
    (ii) areas for food storage, preparation and cooking, and
    (iii) laundry facilities,

which should be available in particular circumstances; and

(b) standards as to the number, type and quality of other facilities or equipment which should be available in particular circumstances.

(5) In this section 'long lease' has the same meaning as in section 61(9).

66 Tests for fitness etc. and satisfactory management arrangements

(1) In deciding for the purposes of section 64(3)(b) or (d) whether a person ('P') is a fit and proper person to be the licence holder or (as the case may be) the manager of the house, the local housing authority must have regard (among other things) to any evidence within subsection (2) or (3).

(2) Evidence is within this subsection if it shows that P has—

(a) committed any offence involving fraud or other dishonesty, or violence or drugs, or any offence listed in Schedule 3 to the *Sexual Offences Act* 2003 (c. 42) (offences attracting notification requirements);

(b) practised unlawful discrimination on grounds of sex, colour, race, ethnic or national origins or disability in, or in connection with, the carrying on of any business;

(c) contravened any provision of the law relating to housing or of landlord and tenant law; or

(d) acted otherwise than in accordance with any applicable code of practice approved under section 233.

(3) Evidence is within this subsection if—

(a) it shows that any person associated or formerly associated with P (whether on a personal, work or other basis) has done any of the things set out in subsection (2)(a) to (d), and

(b) it appears to the authority that the evidence is relevant to the question whether P is a fit and proper person to be the licence holder or (as the case may be) the manager of the house.

(4) For the purposes of section 64(3)(b) the local housing authority must assume, unless the contrary is shown, that the person having control of the house is a more appropriate person to be the licence holder than a person not having control of it.

(5) In deciding for the purposes of section 64(3)(e) whether the proposed management arrangements for the house are otherwise satisfactory, the local housing authority must have regard (among other things) to the considerations mentioned in subsection (6).

(6) The considerations are—
(a) whether any person proposed to be involved in the management of the house has a sufficient level of competence to be so involved;
(b) whether any person proposed to be involved in the management of the house (other than the manager) is a fit and proper person to be so involved; and
(c) whether any proposed management structures and funding arrangements are suitable.

(7) Any reference in section 64(3)(c)(i) or (ii) or subsection (4) above to a person having control of the house, or to being a person of any other description, includes a reference to a person who is proposing to have control of the house, or (as the case may be) to be a person of that description, at the time when the licence would come into force.

67 Licence conditions

(1) A licence may include such conditions as the local housing authority consider appropriate for regulating all or any of the following—
(a) the management, use and occupation of the house concerned, and
(b) its condition and contents.

(1A) For the purposes of section 67(1) a licence may not include a condition that regulates the use, occupation or contents of any part of an HMO unless the condition relates to a matter over which it would be reasonable to expect the licence holder, in all the circumstances, to exercise control.

(2) Those conditions may, in particular, include (so far as appropriate in the circumstances)—
(a) conditions imposing restrictions or prohibitions on the use or occupation of particular parts of the house by persons occupying it;
(b) conditions requiring the taking of reasonable and practicable steps to prevent or reduce anti-social behaviour by persons occupying or visiting the house;

(c)   conditions requiring facilities and equipment to be made available in the house for the purpose of meeting standards prescribed under section 65;

(d)   conditions requiring such facilities and equipment to be kept in repair and proper working order;

(e)   conditions requiring, in the case of any works needed in order for any such facilities or equipment to be made available or to meet any such standards, that the works are carried out within such period or periods as may be specified in, or determined under, the licence;

(f)   conditions requiring the licence holder or the manager of the house to attend training courses in relation to any applicable code of practice approved under section 233.

(3) A licence must include the conditions required by Schedule 4.

(4) As regards the relationship between the authority's power to impose conditions under this section and functions exercisable by them under or for the purposes of Part 1 ('Part 1 functions')—

(a)   the authority must proceed on the basis that, in general, they should seek to identify, remove or reduce category 1 or category 2 hazards in the house by the exercise of Part 1 functions and not by means of licence conditions;

(b)   this does not, however, prevent the authority from imposing licence conditions relating to the installation or maintenance of facilities or equipment within subsection (2)(c) above, even if the same result could be achieved by the exercise of Part 1 functions;

(c)   the fact that licence conditions are imposed for a particular purpose that could be achieved by the exercise of Part 1 functions does not affect the way in which Part 1 functions can be subsequently exercised by the authority.

(5) A licence may not include conditions imposing restrictions or obligations on a particular person other than the licence holder unless that person has consented to the imposition of the restrictions or obligations.

(6) A licence may not include conditions requiring (or intended to secure) any alteration in the terms of any tenancy or licence under which any person occupies the house.

Appendix D

Houses exempted from licensing under Part 3

The following houses are exempt from selective licensing under Part 3, and so cannot be the subject of a special interim management order under s. 103.

- a tenancy or licence of a house or dwelling that is subject to a prohibition order made under s. 20 of the Act whose operation has not been suspended in accordance with s. 23 of the Act;
- a tenancy described in any of the following provisions of Part 1 of Sch. 1 to the *Housing Act* 1988, which cannot be an assured tenancy by virtue of s. 1(2) of that Act—
  - para. 4 (business tenancies);
  - para. 5 (licensed premises);
  - para. 6 (tenancies of agricultural land);
  - para. 7 (tenancies of agricultural holdings etc);
- a tenancy or licence of a house or a dwelling that is managed or controlled by:
  - a local housing authority;
  - a police authority established under s. 3 of the *Police Act* 1996
  - (in England only) the Metropolitan Police Authority established under s. 5B of the *Police Act* 1996;
  - a fire and rescue authority under the *Fire and Rescue Services Act* 2004;
  - a health service body within the meaning of s. 4 of the *National Health Service and Community Care Act* 1990;
- a tenancy or licence of a house which is not a house in multiple occupation for any purposes of the Act (except Part 1) by virtue of either:
  - para. 3 of Sch. 14 to the Act (buildings regulated otherwise than under the Act); or
  - para. 4(1) of that Schedule (buildings occupied by students);
- a tenancy of a house or a dwelling where:
  - the full term of the tenancy is more than 21 years;
  - the lease does not contain a provision enabling the landlord to determine the tenancy, other than by forfeiture, earlier than at end of the term; and

- the house or dwelling is occupied by a person to whom the tenancy was granted or his successor in title or any members of such person's family;
- a tenancy or licence of a house or a dwelling granted by a person to a person who is a member of his family where:
  - the person to whom the tenancy or licence is granted occupies the house or dwelling as his only or main residence;
  - the person granting the tenancy or licence is the freeholder or the holder of a lease of the house or dwelling the full term of which is more than 21 years; and
  - if the person granting the tenancy is the holder of the house or dwelling under a lease, the lease does not contain a provision enabling the landlord to determine the tenancy, other than by forfeiture, earlier than at end of the term;
- a tenancy or licence that is granted to a person in relation to his occupancy of a house or a dwelling as a holiday home;
- a tenancy or licence under the terms of which the occupier shares any accommodation with the landlord or licensor or a member of the landlord's or licensor's family.

Families

For the purposes of these exemptions a person is a member of the same family as another person if they live as a couple; one of them is the relative of the other; or one of them is, or is a relative of, one member of a couple and the other is a relative of the other member of the couple. Here 'couple' means two persons who are married to each other or live together as husband and wife (or in an equivalent relationship in the case of persons of the same sex); 'relative' means parent, grandparent, child, grandchild, brother, sister, uncle, aunt, nephew, niece or cousin; and a relationship of the half-blood is to be treated as a relationship of the whole blood; a stepchild of a person is to be treated as his child.

An occupier shares accommodation with another person if he has the use of an amenity in common with that person (whether or not also in common with others); and 'amenity' includes a toilet, personal washing facilities, a kitchen or a living room but excludes any area used for storage, a staircase , corridor or other means of access.

Appendix E

Prescribed exceptions from the making of an interim EDMO

A dwelling is excepted from the making of an interim EDMO if, under the *Housing (Empty Dwelling Management Orders) (Prescribed Exceptions and Requirements) (Wales) Order* 2006 and the *Housing (Empty Dwelling Management Orders) (Prescribed Exceptions and Requirements) (England) Order*:

- It has been occupied solely or principally by the relevant proprietor and is wholly unoccupied because the relevant proprietor:
  - is temporarily resident elsewhere;
  - is absent from the dwelling for the purpose of receiving personal care by reason of old age, disablement, illness, past or present alcohol or drug dependence or past or present mental disorder;
  - is absent from the dwelling for the purpose of providing, or better providing, personal care for a person who requires such care by reason of old age, disablement, illness, past or present alcohol or drug dependence or past or present mental disorder; or
  - is a serving member of the armed forces and is absent from the dwelling as a result of such service.
- It is used as a holiday home (whether or not it is let as such on a commercial basis) or is otherwise occupied by the relevant proprietor or the relevant proprietor's guests on a temporary basis from time to time.
- It is genuinely on the market for sale or letting.
- It is comprised in an agricultural holding within the meaning of the Agricultural Holdings Act 1986 or a farm business tenancy within the meaning of the Agricultural Tenancies Act 1995.
- It is usually occupied by an employee of the relevant proprietor in connection with the performance of the employee's duties under the terms of the employee's contract of employment.
- It is available for occupation by a minister of religion as a residence from which to perform the duties of the minister of religion's office.

- It is subject to a court order freezing the property of the relevant proprietor.
- It is prevented from being occupied as a result of a criminal investigation or criminal proceedings.
- It is mortgaged, where the mortgagee, in right of the mortgage, has entered into and is in possession of the dwelling.
- The person who was the relevant proprietor of it has died and six months has not elapsed since the grant of representation was obtained in respect of such person.

Appendix F

TDP certificate

Housing Act 2004: Tenancy Deposit Protection

Certificate for compliance with paragraph 2(g) of the Housing (Tenancy Deposits) (Prescribed Information) Order 2007

In compliance with the Housing (Tenancy Deposits) (Prescribed Information) Order 2007 the following information is provided to:

[Tenant(s) Name(s)]

On behalf of:

[Landlord(s) Name(s)]

In relation to the tenancy of:

[Property Address]

From: *[start date]*   **To:** *[end date]*

The name, address, telephone number, facsimile number (if applicable) and email address (if applicable) of any relevant person are attached to this certificate.

The tenant(s) is/are informed that the deposit may be retained by the landlord in accordance with clause(s) *[insert clause numbers]* of the tenancy agreement.

The landlord(s) confirms that all information provided to the tenant(s) in connection with this tenancy is accurate to the best of his knowledge and belief and further confirms that the tenant has been given the opportunity to read and sign all documentation by way of confirmation of this fact.

Signed: **by:**

[if signed on the landlord's behalf]   **of:**

Date:

The tenant(s) confirms that he has been given the opportunity to read and sign this document.

Signed: **Date:**

Appendix G

Residential Property Tribunal offices

London Residential Property Tribunal Service 10 Alfred Place London WC1E 7LR Tel: 0207 446 7700 Fax: 0207 637 1250	All London boroughs
Manchester Residential Property Tribunal Service First Floor 26 York Street Manchester M1 4JB Tel: 0845 100 2614 Fax: 0161 237 3656 or 0161 237 9491	The metropolitan districts of: Bolton, Bury, Manchester, Oldham, Rochdale, Salford, Stockport, Tameside, Trafford, Wigan, Knowsley, Liverpool, St Helens, Sefton, Wirral, Barnsley, Doncaster, Rotherham, Sheffield, Gateshead, Newcastle upon Tyne, North Tyneside, South Tyneside, Sunderland, Bradford, Calderdale, Kirklees, Leeds and Wakefield. The following unitary authorities: Hartlepool, Middlesborough, Redcar and Cleveland, Darlington, Halton, Blackburn with Darwen, Blackpool, Kingston upon Hull, East Riding of Yorkshire, North-east Lincolnshire, North Lincolnshire, Stockton-on-Tees, Warrington and York. The counties of: Cheshire, Cumbria, Durham, Lancashire, Lincolnshire, Northumberland and North Yorkshire.
Midlands Residential Property Tribunal Service 2nd Floor East Wing Ladywood House 45–46 Stephenson Street Birmingham B2 4DH Tel: 0845 100 2615 or 0121 643 8336 Fax: 0121 643 7605	The metropolitan districts of: Birmingham, Coventry, Dudley, Sandwell, Solihull, Walsall, Wolverhampton. The following unitary authorities: Derby, Leicester, Rutland, Nottingham, Herefordshire, Telford and Wrekin and Stoke on Trent. The counties of: Derbyshire, Leicestershire, Nottinghamshire, Shropshire, Staffordshire, Warwickshire and Worcestershire.
Eastern Rent Assessment Panel Great Eastern House Tenison Road Cambridge CB1 2TR Tel: 0845 100 2616 or 0122 3505112 Fax: 01223 505116	The following unitary authorities: Bracknell Forest, West Berkshire, Reading, Slough, Windsor and Maidenhead, Wokingham, Luton, Peterborough, Milton Keynes, Southend on Sea, Thurrock. The counties of: Bedfordshire, Buckinghamshire, Cambridgeshire, Essex, Hertfordshire, Norfolk, Northamptonshire, Oxfordshire and Suffolk.
Southern Rent Assessment Panel 1st Floor 1 Market Avenue Chichester PO19 1JU Tel: 0845 100 2617 or 01243 779394 Fax: 01243 779389	The following unitary authorities: Bath and North-east Somerset, Bristol, North Somerset, South Gloucestershire, Bournemouth, Plymouth, Torbay, Poole, Swindon, Medway, Brighton and Hove, Portsmouth, Southampton and the Isle of Wight. The counties of: Cornwall and the Isles of Scilly, Devon, Dorset, East Sussex, Gloucestershire, Hampshire, Kent, Somerset, Surrey, West Sussex and Wiltshire.

Wales 1st Floor West Wing Southgate House Wood Street Cardiff CF10 1EW	All of Wales

Appendix H

Applications

See tables opposite.

Improvement Notices

specified respondent:	local housing authority			
specified documents:	a copy of the improvement notice (including any schedules to it) the statement of reasons			
type of appeal	**who may appeal**	**additional documents**	**time limit (days)**	**from . . . .**
appeal against improvement notice	person on whom notice is served	where the ground or one of the grounds of the application is that one of the courses of action mentioned in para. 12(2) of Sch. 1 to the Act is the best course of action in relation to the hazard, a statement identifying that course of action with the applicant's reasons for considering it the best course.	21	date on which improvement notice was served
appeal against improvement notice alleging that another person ought to take the action or pay the costs of taking the action	person on whom notice is served	as above plus: the name and address of any person who as an owner of the premises, in the applicant's opinion ought to take the action required by the improvement notice or pay the whole or part of the costs of taking that action ('the other owner') proof of service of a copy of the application on the other owner a statement containing the following details— (i) the nature of the other owner's interest in the premises; (ii) the reason the applicant considers the other owner ought to take the action concerned or pay the whole or part of the cost of taking that action; and (iii) where the ground of the application is that the other owner ought to pay the whole or part of the cost of taking the action, the estimated cost of taking the action and the proportion of that cost which the applicant considers the other owner ought to pay.	21	date on which improvement notice was served
appeal against a decision by authority to vary an improvement notice	person on whom notice is served	a copy of the LHA's decision to vary (including any documentation issued by the LHA in connection with its notice of decision).	28	date when decision to vary was made

	person who applied for the revocation or variation	a copy of the LHA's decision to refuse to vary or revoke (including any documentation issued by the LHA in connection with its notice of decision).	28	date when decision to refuse was made
appeal against a decision by authority to refuse to vary or revoke an improvement notice	person who applied for the revocation or variation	a copy of the LHA's decision to refuse to vary or revoke (including any documentation issued by the LHA in connection with its notice of decision).	28	date when decision to refuse was made
appeal against a demand by authority for recovery of expenses incurred by LHA in taking action where improvement notice has been served	person on whom demand was served	a copy of the notice served by the LHA under para. 4 of Sch. 3 to the Act (notice of LHA's intention to enter premises to carry out specified actions without agreement); a copy of the LHA's demand for expenses; and where the application is made on the ground mentioned in para. 11(4) of that Schedule, details of the progress relied upon as being made towards compliance with the notice.	21	service of the demand

Prohibition orders

specified respondent	local housing authority unless otherwise stated below			
specified documents	a copy of the prohibition order (including any schedules to it) the statement of reasons			
type of appeal	**who may appeal**	**additional documents**	**time limit (days)**	**from . . . .**
appeal against LHA's refusal to give approval of particular use under s. 22(4)	person applying for approval	notice of the LHA's decision to refuse a particular use of the whole or part of the premises.	28	date of decision by authority
application by lessor or lessee for order determining or varying lease where a prohibition order has become operative	lessor or lessee	a copy of the relevant lease; and a statement of the name and address of any other party to the lease and of any party to an inferior lease *specified respondent is 'other party to the lease'*	None	

| appeal against a prohibition order | anyone who is an owner or occupier of the whole or part of the specified premises, anyone authorised to permit persons to occupy the whole or part of those premises any mortgagee of the whole or part of those premises. | where one of the grounds of the application is that one of the courses of action mentioned in para. 8(2) of Sch. 2 to the Act is the best course of action in relation to the hazard, a statement identifying that course of action with the applicant's reasons for considering it the best course. | 28 | date on which order was made |
| appeal against a decision of the housing authority to vary or to refuse to vary or revoke a prohibition order | as above | a copy of the LHA's decision to vary or refuse to vary or revoke (including any documentation issued by the LHA in connection with its notice of decision). | 28 | date on which decision concerned was made |

Emergency Remedial Action				
appeal against decision of authority to take emergency remedial action has been served	person on whom notice has been served	a copy of the notice of emergency remedial action (including any schedule to it) the statement of reasons. *Specified respondent: the local housing authority*	28 days	date specified in the notice as the date when action was (or will be) started
appeal against an emergency prohibition order	'relevant person'	copy of the notice of emergency prohibition order made under s. 43 of the Act (including any schedule to it); and the statement of reasons. *Specified respondent: the local housing authority*	28 days	date on which order was made
application by LHA for order for recovery of expenses and interest from person profiting from the taking of action without agreement	local housing authority	a copy of the notice of emergency remedial action (including any schedule to it) the statement of reasons; a copy of the demand for expenses a copy of any recovery notice proof of service of notice of the application on the person concerned. *Specified respondent: the person from whom the Local Housing Authority seeks recovery of expenses*	None	None
an appeal against a demand by the LHA for recovery of expenses incurred by taking emergency remedial action	person on who the demand was served	a copy of the notice of emergency remedial action the statement of reasons a copy of the notice of LHA's intention to enter premises to carry out specified actions without agreement a copy of the LHA's demand for expenses where the application is made on the ground that reasonable compliance was being made with an improvement notice, details of the progress relied upon as being made towards compliance with the notice.	21 days	date of service of demand

Demolition Orders				
specified documents		Note: in this table 'owner' includes any leaseholder with a term of more than three years and any person entitled to sell the freehold (except for a mortgagee in possession).		
Appeal by a person aggrieved by a demolition order	anyone aggrieved by the order, but not someone in occupation under an agreement or lease of more than three years	a copy of the demolition order with any schedules to it the statement of reasons; where the ground or one of the grounds of the application is that one of the courses of action mentioned in s. 269A(2) of the 1985 Act is the best course of action in relation to the hazard, a statement identifying that course of action with the applicant's reasons for considering it the best course. *Specified respondent: the local housing authority*	21 days	service of the demolition order
application for recovery of authority's expenses or determination of contribution by joint owners	local housing authority or joint owner	a statement of— (i) the expenses incurred by the Local Housing Authority in executing the demolition order; (ii) the amount (if any) realised by the sale of materials; and (iii) the amount the LHA seeks to recover from an owner of the premises. *Specified respondent: the owner of the premises (see head of table for definition of owner)*	6 years	liability to pay expenses arising
application by an owner of premises for determination of contribution ot LHA's expenses to be paid by another owner	owner of the premises	a statement of— (i) the owners' respective interests in the premises; and (ii) their respective obligations and liabilities in respect of maintenance and repair under any covenant or agreement, whether express or implied. *Specified respondent: the owner from whom the applicant seeks a contribution to the local housing authority's expenses*	6 years	liability to pay expenses arising
application by lessor or lessee of premises for an order determining the lease		a copy of the relevant lease a statement of the name and address of any other party to the lease and of any party to an inferior lease. *Specified respondent: the other party to the lease*	6 years	date of the making of the demolition order

Work on unfit premises			
application by person with interest in premises for authorisation by tribunal of execution of works on unfit premises or for improvement	a person entitled to any interest in the land	details of the work which the applicant proposes to carry out including— (i) names and addresses of proposed contractors where relevant; (ii) an estimate of the costs of the work; and (iii) a timetable for starting and completing the work; where the application is made on the ground mentioned in s. 318(1)(b) of the 1985 Act, details of— (i) the scheme of improvement or reconstruction which the applicant wishes to carry out; and (ii) the LHA's approval of the scheme. a statement of the financial standing of the applicant including disclosure of funds available to meet the estimated costs of the work; where the application includes a request for an order determining a lease held from the applicant or a derivative lease, a copy of that lease. *The specified respondents are—* *(a) the person with a right to possession of the premises;* *(b) the owner of the premises*	No time limit given	N/A

HMO licensing				
appeal against refusal by LHA to serve a temporary exemption notice	person who applied for the temporary exemption notice	a copy of the notification to the LHA under s. 62(1) of the Act; a copy of the LHA's decision notice under s. 62(6) of the Act. *Specified respondent: the LHA.*	28 days	date of LHA's decision to refuse
application by LHA for rent repayment order	LHA	(i) copy of the notice of intending proceedings under s. 73(7); (ii) a copy of any representation received in respect of the notice; (iii) either— (a) a statement containing the details relied on in making the allegation that an offence under section 72(1) of the Act was committed; or (b) where the LHA relies on the provisions of section 74 of the Act, proof that the appropriate person has been convicted of an offence under section 72(1) of the Act; and (iv) a document showing the housing benefit paid by the LHA in connection with occupation of the premises during the period in which it is alleged such an offence was committed. *Specified respondent: the 'appropriate person'*	No time limit is given – presumably there is a 6 year time limit from the date of payment of the Housing Benefit, under the Limitation Act 1980.	
application by occupier for rent repayment order	person who occupied the property while it was unlicensed	evidence that the appropriate person has been convicted of an offence under s. 72(1) of the Act or has been required by a rent repayment order to make a repayment of housing benefit; and evidence that the occupier has paid periodical payments (e.g. rent) in respect of occupation of the premises during a period which it is alleged that such an offence was being committed. *Specified respondent: the 'appropriate person'*	12 months	whichever is the later of the date of conviction or the date on which a rent repayment order was made to the LHA
appeal against decision of LHA to serve an HMO declaration	any 'relevant person'	a copy of the HMO declaration. *Specified respondent: the local housing authority*	28 days	authority's decision

appeal against decision of LHA to refuse to revoke HMO declaration	'relevant person' who applied to the LHA to have the HMO declaration revoked	a copy of the HMO declaration a copy of the LHA's notice of decision not to revoke the HMO declaration. *Specified respondent: the local housing authority*	28 days	authority's decision
appeal against decision by LHA to grant, an HMO licence or against any of the terms of the licence	person who applied for the licence or any 'relevant person'	a copy of the LHA's notices under paras 1 and 7 of Sch. 5, and of any notice under para. 3 of that Schedule; and a copy of the licence. *Specified respondent: the local housing authority*	28 days	decision to grant the licence was made
appeal against decision by LHA to refuse to grant, an HMO licence	person who applied for the licence or any 'relevant person'	a copy of the LHA's notices under paras 5 and 8 of Sch. 5 *Specified respondent: the local housing authority*	28 days	decision to refuse to grant the licence was made
appeal by licence holder or any relevant person against decision by LHA with regard to the variation or revocation of licence	licence holder or any 'relevant person'	a copy of the licence, and one of the following: where the application relates to a decision to vary a licence, a copy of the LHA's notices under paras 14 and 16 of Sch. 5; where the application relates to refusal to vary a licence, a copy of the LHA's notices under paras 19 and 21 of that Schedule; where the application relates to a decision to revoke a licence, a copy of the LHA's notices under paras 22 and 24 of that Schedule; where the application relates to refusal to revoke a licence, a copy of the LHA's notices under paras 26 and 28 of that Schedule. *Specified respondent: the local housing authority*	28 days	authority's decision to vary or revoke

Selective licensing

appeal against refusal by LHA to serve a temporary exemption notice	person who applied for the temporary exemption notice	a copy of the notification to the LHA / a copy of the LHA's decision notice / *Specified respondent: the LHA.*	28 days	date of LHA's decision to refuse
application by LHA for rent repayment order	LHA	copy of the notice of intending proceedings / a copy of any representation received in respect of the notice; / a document showing the housing benefit paid by the LHA in connection with occupation of the premises during the period in which it is alleged such an offence was committed / either— / (a) a statement containing the details relied on in making the allegation that an offence under s. 95(1) of the Act was committed; or / (b) where the LHA relies on the provisions of s. 97 of the Act, proof that the appropriate person has been convicted of an offence under s. 95(1) of the Act / *Specified respondent: the 'appropriate person'*	No time limit is given – presumably there is a six-year time limit from the date of payment of the Housing Benefit, under the Limitation Act 1980.	application by LHA for rent repayment order
application by occupier for rent repayment order	person who occupied the property while it was unlicensed	evidence that the appropriate person has been convicted of an offence under s. 95(1) of the Act or has been required by a rent repayment order to make a repayment of housing benefit; and / evidence that the occupier has paid periodical payments (e.g. rent) in respect of occupation of the premises during a period which it is alleged that such an offence was being committed. / *Specified respondent: the 'appropriate person'*	12 months	whichever is the later of the date of conviction or the date on which a rent repayment order was made to the LHA
appeal against decision by LHA to grant, a selective residential licence or against any of the terms of the licence	person who applied for the licence or any 'relevant person'	a copy of the LHA's notices under paras 1 and 7 of Sch. 5, and of any notice under para. 3 of that Schedule; and / a copy of the licence / *Specified respondent: the local housing authority*	28 days	decision to grant the licence was made

	person who applied for the licence or any 'relevant person'	a copy of the LHA's notices under paras 5 and 8 of Sch. 5 *Specified respondent: the local housing authority*	28 days	decision to refuse to grant the licence was made
appeal against decision by LHA to refuse to grant, a selective residential licence				
appeal by licence holder or any relevant person against decision by LHA with regard to the variation or revocation of licence	licence holder or any 'relevant person'	a copy of the licence, and one of the following: where the application relates to a decision to vary a licence, a copy of the LHA's notices under paras 14 and 16 of Sch. 5; where the application relates to refusal to vary a licence, a copy of the LHA's notices under paras 19 and 21 of that Schedule; where the application relates to a decision to revoke a licence, a copy of the LHA's notices under paras 22 and 24 of that Schedule; where the application relates to refusal to revoke a licence, a copy of the LHA's notices under paras 26 and 28 of that Schedule. *Specified respondent: thelocal housing authority*	28 days	authority's decision to vary or revoke

Interim and Final Management Orders			No time limit applies
LHA application for authorisation to make an Interim Management Order	LHA	a copy of the draft order a statement of matters relevant to the tribunal's consideration of— (i) whether the health and safety condition in section 104 of the Act is satisfied; and (ii) the extent to which any applicable code of practice approved under s. 233 of the Act has been complied with; and (iii) where the LHA requests that the application be dealt with as a matter of urgency under reg. 9, a statement giving sufficient details to enable the tribunal to form an opinion as to whether the exceptional circumstances mentioned in para. (3) of that regulation appear to exist. *Specified respondent: a 'relevant person'.*	No time limit applies
LHA application for authorisation to make a Special Interim Management Order (SIMO)	LHA	a copy of the draft order; a statement of matters relevant to the tribunal's consideration as to whether the conditions in s. 103(3) and (4) are satisfied; and where the LHA requests that the application be dealt with as a matter of urgency under reg. 9, a statement giving sufficient details to enable the tribunal to form an opinion as to whether the exceptional circumstances mentioned in para. (3) of that regulation appear to exist. *Specified respondent: a 'relevant person'*	No time limit applies
LHA application for order that an Interim Management Order continue in force pending disposal of appeal)	LHA	a copy of the interim management order a copy of the notice of appeal *Specified respondent: the person who made the appeal*	No time limit applies

application by relevant landlord for order regarding financial arrangements while Interim Management Order in force	immediate landlord of the whole or part of the property	a copy of the interim management order; a copy of the accounts kept by the LHA in accordance with s. 110(6). *Specified respondent: the Local Housing Authority*	while Interim Manage-ment Order is in force / N/A
LHA application for order that existing Final Management Order continue in force pending disposal of appeal against new Final Management Order	LHA	a copy of the existing final Management Order; a copy of the new Final Management Order made in order to replace it; and a copy of the notice of appeal under para. 24 of Sch. 6 to the Act against the making of the new Final Management Order. *Specified respondent: the person who made the appeal*	
application by an affected person for order that LHA manage in accordance with management scheme in Final Management Order	'relevant landlord' or a third party to whom compensation is payable	a copy of the Final Management Order which contains the management scheme to which the application relates. *Specified respondent: the local housing authority*	N/A / N/A
application for adjustment of rights and liabilities with regard to furniture vested in LHA while Management Order in force	anyone against whom the rights of the authority is exercisable	a copy of the relevant Management Order; and a statement giving details of the respective rights and liabilities (including ownership) of the persons interested in the furniture. *Specified respondent: the other person interested in the furniture*	N/A / N/A

application to determine who is 'the relevant landlord' for the purposes of s. 130 on termination of Management Order	any 'relevant landlord'	a copy of the Management Order. *Specified respondent: the other relevant landlord*	N/A	N/A
appeal against making of a Management Order, or against the terms of the order or of associated management scheme	'relevant person'	a copy of the Management Order (including the management scheme); a copy of the notice served by the LHA under para. 7(2)(b) of Sch. 6 to the Act; where the application relates to the terms of the Management Order, a statement specifying each term to which objection is made, with reasons for the objection; and where the application is made on the ground specified in para. 24(3) of Sch. 6 to the Act, a statement of the matters in s. 110(5)(which relates to payments of surplus rents etc) relevant to that ground. *Specified respondent: the local housing authority*	28 days	making of the order
appeal against LHA's decision or refusal to vary or revoke Management Order	'relevant person'	a copy of the Management Order; and a copy of the notice served by the LHA under para. 7(2)(b) of Sch. 6 to the Act. and one of the following: where the application relates to a decision to vary a Management Order, a copy of the LHA's notices under paras 9 and 11 of Sch. 6; where the application relates to refusal to vary a Management Order, a copy of the LHA's notices under paras 14 and 16 of that Schedule; where the application relates to a decision to revoke a Management Order, a copy of the LHA's notices under paras 17 and 19 of that Schedule; and where the application relates to refusal to revoke a Management Order, a copy of the LHA's notices under paras 20 and 22 of that Schedule. *Specified respondent: the local housing authority*	28 days	authority's decision

| appeal by third party against LHA's decision under s. 128 of the Act regarding compensation payable to third parties | third party about whom the decision was made | a copy of the Management Order (including the management scheme); a copy of the LHA's notification of its decision to the third party in accordance with s. 128(2) of the Act; and a statement giving full details of—
(i) the rights in respect of which it is claimed that there has been interference in consequence of the Management Order; and
(ii) the amount of compensation claimed in respect of that interference.
Specified respondent: the local housing authority | 28 days | notifi-cation of the decision to the third party |

Empty Dwelling Management Orders				
LHA application for authorisation to make interim EDMO	LHA	a copy of the draft interim EDMO; a statement of evidence— (i) in respect of the matters as to which the tribunal must be satisfied under s. 134(2) of the Act; (ii) of the LHA's consideration of the rights and interests specified in s. 133(4) of the Act; and where the LHA in accordance with s. 133(3) of the Act notified the relevant proprietor that it was considering making an interim EDMO, a copy of the notification. *Specified respondent: the 'relevant proprietor'*	N/A	N/A
application while interim EDMO in force for order that the LHA pay compensation to third party for interference with rights	third party	a copy of the interim EDMO (including the management scheme); a copy of the LHA's notification of its decision to the third party in accordance with s. 138(4) of the Act; and a statement giving full details of— (i) the rights in respect of which it is claimed that there has been interference in consequence of the interim EDMO; and (ii) the amount of compensation claimed in respect of that interference. *Specified respondent: the local housing authority*	while the EDMO is in force	N/A
LHA application for order that interim EDMO continue in force pending disposal of appeal under para. 26 of that Schedule	LHA	a copy of the interim EDMO; and a copy of the notice of appeal under para. 26 of Sch. 7 to the Act against the making of an interim EDMO. *Specified respondent: the person who made the pending appeal*	N/A	N/A

LHA's application for order under para. 22 of that Schedule determining a lease or licence while interim or final EDMO is in force	LHA	a copy of the interim or final EDMO (including any management scheme); a copy of the relevant lease or licence, or if not available evidence of the existence of the lease or licence; and a statement containing the following details— (i) the name and address where known of any lessor, lessee, sub-lessor, sub-lessee or licensee; (ii) evidence of matters in respect of which the tribunal must be satisfied under para. 22(1)(b) of Sch. 7 to the Act; and (iii) the amount of compensation (if any) which the LHA is willing to pay in respect of the determination of the lease or licence, including details of how such compensation has been calculated. *Specified respondents: the parties to the lease or licence.*	N/A	N/A
application by relevant proprietor for order in connection with financial arrangements while interim EDMO in force	'relevant proprietor'	a copy of the interim EDMO; and a copy of the accounts kept by the LHA in accordance with para. 5(6) of Sch. 7 to the Act. *Specified respondent: the Local Housing Authority*	while interim EDMO is in force	N/A
application by LHA for order that final EDMO should continue in force pending disposal of an appeal under para. 26	LHA	a copy of the interim EDMO (so the regulations state but they must mean the 'final EDMO') a copy of the notice of appeal under para. 26 of Sch. 7 to the Act against the making of a final EDMO. *Specified respondent: the person who made the pending appeal.*	No time limit	No time limit

			N/A	N/A
application by a affected person for order that LHA manage dwelling in accordance with management scheme in final EDMO	'relevant proprietor' or a third party to whom compensation is payable or a lessor, lessee, licensor or licensee under a lease or licence terminated by an order of the residential property tribunal and to whom compensation is payable for that termination	a copy of the final EDMO (including the management scheme). *Specified respondent: the local housing authority*		
appeal against LHA's decision to make final EDMO or against terms of the order or of associated management scheme	'relevant person'	a copy of the final EDMO (including the management scheme); where the application relates to the terms of the management order, a statement specifying each term to which objection is made, with reasons for the objection where the application is made on the ground specified in para. 26(1)(c) of Sch. 6 to the Act, a statement of the matters in para. 5(5)(a) and (b)(which relate to payments of surplus rents etc) relevant to that ground. *Specified respondent: the local housing authority*	28 days	making of the order

			28 days	date of decision
appeal against LHA's decision or refusal to vary or revoke interim or final EDMO	'relevant person'	a copy of the interim or final EDMO (as the case may be). one of: where the application relates to a decision to vary an interim or final EDMO, a copy of the LHA's notices under paras 9 and 11 of Sch. 6 to the Act (as applied by para. 17 of Sch. 7); where the application relates to refusal to vary an interim or final EDMO, a copy of the LHA's notices under paras 14 and 16 of that Schedule; where the application relates to a decision to revoke an interim or final EDMO, a copy of the LHA's notices under paras 17 and 19 of that Schedule; and where the application relates to refusal to revoke an interim or final EDMO, a copy of the LHA's notices under paras 20 and 22 of that Schedule. *Specified respondent: the local housing authority*		
appeal against LHA's decision concerning compensation payable to third parties for interference with rights in consequence of final EDMO	any third party	a copy of the final EDMO (including the management scheme); a statement giving full details of— (i) the rights in respect of which it is claimed that there has been interference in consequence of the final EDMO; and (ii) the amount of compensation claimed in respect of that interference. *Specified respondent: the local housing authority*	28 days	making of the order
appeal against LHA's decision under s. 138(3) of the Act in respect of compensation payable to third parties for interference with rights in consequence of final EDMO	the requesting party	a copy of the final EDMO (including the management scheme); a copy of the LHA's notification of its decision to the third party in accordance with subs. (4) of that section; and a statement giving full details of— (i) the rights in respect of which it is claimed that there has been interference in consequence of the final EDMO; and (ii) the amount of compensation claimed in respect of that interference. *Specified respondent: the local housing authority*	28 days	date on which the authority notified the requesting party

Overcrowding Notices				
appeal against making of an Overcrowding Notice	a person aggrieved	a copy of the Overcrowding Notice, or a statement by the applicant explaining the circumstances by reason of which he is not able to provide a copy of this notice.	21 days	service of the notice
appeal by relevant person against LHA's refusal to revoke or vary an overcrowding notice, or against failure by the LHA to respond in time to an application to revoke or vary it	person who applied to the LHA	a copy of the Overcrowding Notice; where the LHA refused to vary an Overcrowding Notice, a copy of the LHA's decision.	21 days	the later of: date on which applicant is notified by LHA of refusal 35 days after application was made (if LHA fail to respond in time).

Index